CREATIVE
S·T·E·A·M
CUISINE

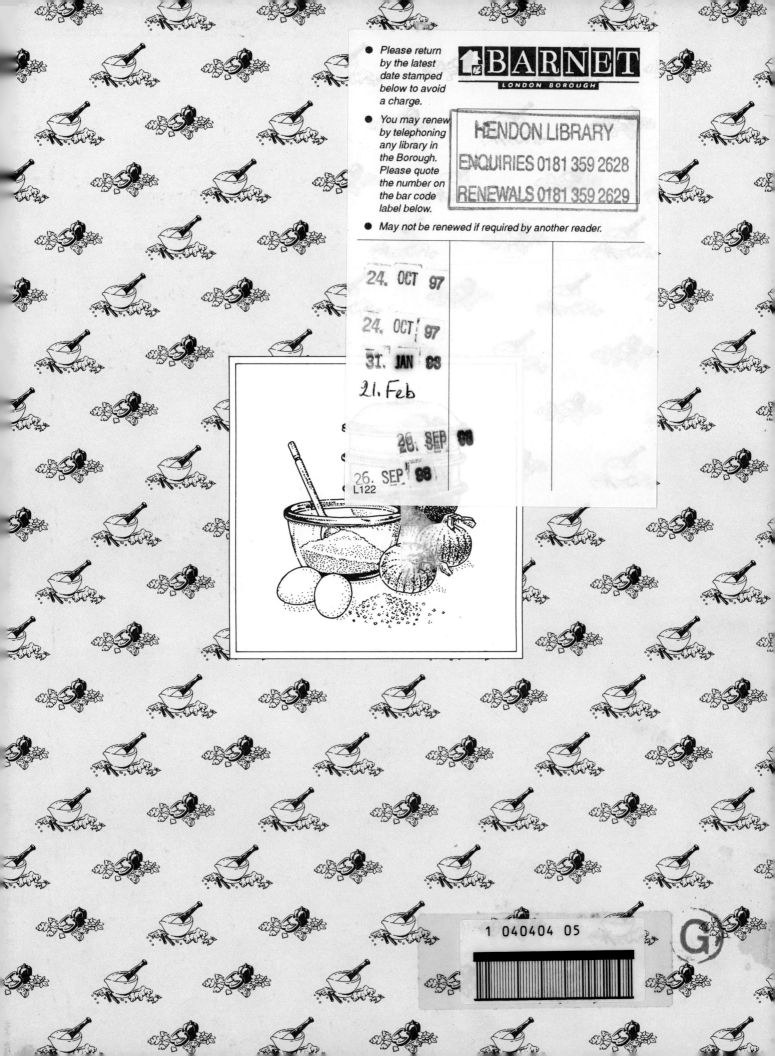

CREATIVE S·T·E·A·M CUISINE

KATE BENSON

HAMLYN

Photography by Clive Streeter
Line drawings by Jane Cradock-Watson
Jacket background reproduced from Cloud Nine Storm
Grey in the Robert Horne Colour Collection.

Published by The Hamlyn Publishing Group Limited
Michelin House, 81 Fulham Road
London SW3 6RB

First published 1988

ISBN 0 600 55545 3

Set in Monophoto Optima by
Tameside Filmsetting, Ltd.
Printed by Mandarin Offset Hong Kong

The publishers would like to thank Vivalp U.K. Ltd.
for lending their Electric Steam Cooker for testing purposes.

CONTENTS

USEFUL FACTS & FIGURES

Notes on metrication

In this book quantities are given in metric and Imperial measures. Exact conversion from Imperial to metric measures does not usually give very convenient working quantities and so the metric measures have been rounded off into units of 25 grams. The table below shows the recommended equivalents.

Ounces	Approx g to nearest whole figure	Recommended conversion to nearest unit of 25	Ounces	Approx g to nearest whole figure	Recommended conversion to nearest unit of 25
1	28	25	9	255	250
2	57	50	10	283	275
3	85	75	11	312	300
4	113	100	12	340	350
5	142	150	13	368	375
6	170	175	14	396	400
7	198	200	15	425	425
8	227	225	16 (1 lb)	454	450

Note: When converting quantities over 16 oz first add the appropriate figures in the centre column, then adjust to the nearest unit of 25. As a general guide, 1 kg (1000 g) equals 2.2 lb or about 2 lb 3 oz. This method of conversion gives good results in nearly all cases, although in certain pastry and cake recipes a more accurate conversion is necessary to produce a balanced recipe.

Liquid measures The millilitre has been used in this book and the following table gives a few examples.

Imperial	Approx ml to nearest whole figure	Recommended ml	Imperial	Approx ml to nearest whole figure	Recommended ml
$\frac{1}{4}$ pint	142	150 ml	1 pint	567	600 ml
$\frac{1}{2}$ pint	283	300 ml	$1\frac{1}{2}$ pints	851	900 ml
$\frac{3}{4}$ pint	425	450 ml	$1\frac{3}{4}$ pints	992	1000 ml (1 litre)

Spoon measures All spoon measures given in this book are level unless otherwise stated.

Can sizes At present, cans are marked with the exact (usually to the nearest whole number) metric equivalent of the Imperial weight of the contents, so we have followed this practice when giving can sizes.

Oven temperatures

The table below gives recommended equivalents.

	°C	°F	Gas Mark		°C	°F	Gas Mark
Very cool	110	225	$\frac{1}{4}$	Moderately hot	190	375	5
	120	250	$\frac{1}{2}$		200	400	6
Cool	140	275	1	Hot	220	425	7
	150	300	2		230	450	8
Moderate	160	325	3	Very hot	240	475	9
	180	350	4				

Notes for American and Australian users

In America the 8-fl oz measuring cup is used. In Australia metric measures are now used in conjunction with the standard 250-ml measuring cup. The Imperial pint, used in Britain and Australia, is 20 fl oz, while the American pint is 16 fl oz. It is important to remember that the Australian tablespoon differs from both the British and American tablespoons; the table below gives a comparison. The British standard tablespoon, which has been used throughout this book, holds 17.7 ml, the American 14.2 ml, and the Australian 20 ml. A teaspoon holds approximately 5 ml in all three countries.

British	American	Australian
1 teaspoon	1 teaspoon	1 teaspoon
1 tablespoon	1 tablespoon	1 tablespoon
2 tablespoons	3 tablespoons	2 tablespoons
$3\frac{1}{2}$ tablespoons	4 tablespoons	3 tablespoons
4 tablespoons	5 tablespoons	$3\frac{1}{2}$ tablespoons

An Imperial/American guide to solid and liquid measures

Imperial	American	Imperial	American
Solid measures		**Liquid measures**	
1 lb butter or		$\frac{1}{4}$ pint liquid	$\frac{2}{3}$ pint liquid
margarine	2 cups	$\frac{1}{2}$ pints	$1\frac{1}{4}$ cups
1 lb flour	4 cups	$\frac{3}{4}$ pint	2 cups
1 lb granulated or		1 pint	$2\frac{1}{2}$ cups
caster sugar	2 cups	$1\frac{1}{2}$ pints	$3\frac{3}{4}$ cups
1 lb icing sugar	3 cups	2 pints	5 cups
8 oz rice	1 cup		($2\frac{1}{2}$ pints)

All of the recipes are for 4 people unless otherwise stated.

FOREWORD

In my opinion, the essential prerequisite for good cooking is the cook's appreciation of good food. Cooking is not a difficult art, but like any art it needs practice to gain experience: so if you can read a recipe, have a bit of enthusiasm, and don't mind experimenting on yourself or on unsuspecting friends, then you're well on the way to becoming an excellent and confident cook.

There are a few basic rules that you should follow at all times. The first trick to learn is to plan ahead and to be well organised. Read the recipes that you are planning to use through thoroughly, and give yourself adequate time for marinating, preparation, and cooking. It would be rather unfortunate to discover that you need several hours to marinate some of the ingredients when your guests are due in only 5 minutes time!

Another important point is to use proper stock. Reduced stock – stock that has been boiled to make the flavour more concentrated – is infinitely preferable for use as the base of a sauce to salty packet stock-cubes which are a poor substitute for the real thing.

It has to be better to use fresh rather than frozen foods, so exploit seasonal ingredients to the full. Check the Glossary of Ingredients (page 121) of this book for information about when food is in season.

The appearance of food should neither surprise your guests, nor should you want to frame it forever! You should want to tuck in immediately because it looks so good, but beware of too much fussiness in the preparation of the food.

The main purpose of this book is to introduce you to the relative merits of steaming as a method of cooking, and to show you some of the many ideas that you might want to use. As you pick up the techniques, then you will be able to experiment with exciting new ideas of your own. However to start you off every recipe in this book has been fully tested, and my guests and I thoroughly enjoyed trying them.

If there is one point I would particularly like to emphasise, it is to use proper stock when making sauces. It is so tempting to cut corners and use cubes or powder, but that little extra effort really works wonders.

I would like to thank Sandra Allen and Jane Cusack who spent many hours deciphering my writing, and typing the manuscript, and most of all am indebted to my husband Harry who has helped and encouraged me throughout.

All of my recipes should be simple and easy to follow so now there is no excuse for not producing good-looking, good-tasting, healthy (and sometimes not so healthy!) food and having the satisfaction of seeing the smiling faces on your own well-fed guests.

Happy steaming!

Kate Benoc

INTRODUCTION TO STEAMING

Steaming used to be a very popular method of cooking in the old days when many households had servants or wives at home with plenty of time on their hands. Steamed sweet and savoury puddings were particularly common then. However as people started to lead faster and more active lives, and more women had to go off to work during the day, then it was the fast-cooking and easy-to-prepare methods, such as frying, grilling, and more recently microwave cooking, which seemed to take over from the more traditional slower methods.

Nowadays, the promotion of health and convenience is the major feature of modern cuisine so, as an apparently 'slow and relatively unhealthy' form of cooking, why has steaming become so popular?

There are three methods of steaming. The first is a quick method of cooking meat, fish, or vegetables by suspending them over the direct steam produced from boiling water below. This is the most popular method of steaming used today and has a number of advantages over other cooking methods: the food is kept stationary so that it cooks gently with little possibility for breaking up; the steam dissolves far less of the colour, flavour and goodness of the food than other methods; and if you use proper stock, court-

bouillon, or any other aromatic infusion instead of boiling water, then you both add flavour and nutrients to the steamed food as well as end up with the base for a delicious sauce.

The second method of steaming is the traditional prolonged way of cooking sealed sweet and savoury puddings in a basin over or in boiling liquid where the food steams in its own juice, and the boiling liquid or its steam does not come into contact with the actual food. This is much the same as placing the sealed pudding in the oven, except that steaming guarantees an exact temperature and evenly spread heat.

The third method of steaming is the oriental classic method of steaming rice, where the rice is washed well and immersed in water. For best results, make sure that the level of water is no higher than 2.5 cm/1 in above the top of the rice. Bring the water to the boil, then reduce the heat to the lowest possible setting, cover with a tight-fitting lid and allow the rice to steam for 15–20 minutes.

There are four golden rules to remember when steaming:

1. The first is to make sure that the steamer is covered with a tight-fitting lid to prevent the steam and any escaping nutrients from getting out, although some leaking is inevitable.

2. Secondly you must ensure that the liquid level in the saucepan does not touch the base of the steamer above, otherwise the food will not be steaming but boiling, and you will end up with a stodgy mush.

3. Thirdly the liquid below must not boil dry, or you will find that your once delicious stock will now be dried, burnt, and forever welded to the saucepan, AND your cooking times for the steamed food will become mere guesswork! It is a good idea to have simmering stock or water ready to one side for addition when necessary, and you must check the liquid level regularly, ideally every 10–15 minutes.

4. Finally, the heat of the steam is so intense that even when you turn the cooker off, the food will continue to cook unless you remove it from the steamer immediately. It is also important to either serve straight away, or cover with foil and keep warm, in order to prevent all the nutrients and flavour from escaping.

STEAMERS

There are many different shapes and sizes of steamer available, but all of them follow the same basic principles.

There are three essential parts to a steaming set. The first is the bottom compartment which contains the boiling liquid: this is usually either a saucepan or wok. On top of this goes the steaming compartment, or steamer, which contains the food to be cooked: this is simply a container with holes or perforations in its base that allow the steam to circulate through. Often more than one steaming compartment can be stacked on the base. Finally a lid is needed to seal the whole system as completely as possible, although some leaking because of heat and pressure is inevitable.

The best variety is the large purpose-built steamer which will usually have two, three or more layers composing the top compartment so that meat and vegetables can be separately steamed at the same time. This type of steamer is available in the form of a work-top electric appliance. A thermostatically controlled element is located beneath the base compartment to heat the water or liquid. The steaming compartments provide plenty of space for steaming at least two layers of food and a neat-fitting domed lid ensures the maximum amount of steam stays in the containers as well as providing plenty of height for accommodating basins or large poultry.

This process is exactly the same as with traditional Chinese bamboo steamers where many of the pretty round baskets can be snugly fitted on top of each other and then sealed with a tight bamboo lid: this tower is then rather precariously placed on a wok filled with boiling water, and the steam circulates inside to cook all of the different foods.

The wok is a perfect implement for use in steaming as you can simply put the food on a wire rack over boiling water inside, and then cover with a tall dome-like lid and leave to steam. The North Africans use a couscoussier – a large pot with a steamer on top – for steaming their traditional dish, couscous (see Pasta, Pulses & Grains chapter).

Perhaps the two most common, cheap and easy-to-use steamers are first the simple aluminium steamer with graduated ridges on its base rim, and second the expanding steel basket, which is made of overlapping steel plates set on short legs. Both of these are flexible enough to fit a whole range of different-sized saucepans.

IMPROVISING

If a recipe sounds particularly delicious but you don't have a smart set of steamers, then don't worry! Yet another of the beauties of steaming is that you can improvise.

For the conventional method, balance a colander or sieve inside a saucepan and cover with foil or wet towels as a lid; or use a deep roasting tin two-thirds full of water with a wire rack just above the water. Place the food on the rack, and then cover with a large dome of foil or greaseproof paper that is tightly sealed at the edges. This method of steaming is one to use when cooking long fish or other similarly large items of food.

For the covered 'pudding basin' method, place a small wire rack or inverted heat proof plate in a large saucepan to stop the basin touching the bottom. Put the covered basin inside and then half-fill the saucepan with boiling water. Simply add a tight lid to the saucepan and steam away! Make sure that the saucepan is big enough to allow the steam to circulate properly around the top of the basin.

Finally if just steaming food in its own juices, you could use two suitable plates, one inverted on top of the other, with the food sandwiched in between, and simply place on top of a saucepan. The bottom plate acts as a lid to prevent the water from boiling away, and the top plate seals in the steam produced by heating the food.

FISH & SEAFOOD

Fish is one of the highest sources of protein available, and has the added advantage of being low in fat and carbohydrates. Any fat contained in fish is polyunsaturated, unlike animal fat which is saturated. Increased health consciousness and the fine nutritional qualities of fish have led to a much-deserved renaissance for this excellent food. There is also great enjoyment to be had in selecting from the wealth of form and colour represented by fish and seafood; from the distinctively coloured plaice, to the attractive fan-shaped scallop shell, a fishmonger's display is a positive inspiration. Steaming is the most effective method for preserving nutritional content and flavour when cooking fish. This chapter includes all sorts of fish, and the reader is encouraged to experiment by substituting favourite seafoods for the fish and shellfish suggested in the recipes.

Scallop Brochette (page 20)

BASIC FISH STOCK

You will see in the recipes which follow that fish stock often plays the important role of well-flavoured sauce base. Stock can be made in advance, if preferred, and kept in the refrigerator, or stored in the freezer in an ice-cube tray.

▶ Place all ingredients in a large saucepan or stock pot. Cover with water and bring to the boil. Simmer for 20–30 minutes, occasionally skimming. *Do not leave the stock to simmer for more than 30 minutes as the bones become bitter.*

Strain through a cloth or fine sieve, allowing it to drip. To strengthen the stock, bring back to the boil and boil rapidly to reduce.

Season with salt, pepper and lemon juice.

1 small onion, roughly sliced
1 small carrot, roughly sliced
1 celery stick, roughly chopped
1 small leek, trimmed, washed and roughly sliced (optional)
fish bones, trimmings and crustacean shells, broken up
2–3 parsley stalks · 1 bay leaf
pinch of chopped fresh herbs, for example, dill, fennel leaves or thyme
mushroom trimmings (optional)
salt and freshly ground black pepper
lemon juice

STEAMED FISH WITH FRESH GARDEN HERBS

I tested this recipe using a fresh grey mullet and the result was succulent and delicious. Feel free to use any whole fish such as bream, John Dory, brill or salmon trout. Follow my recipe exactly, weigh the fish and calculate the steaming time at 10 minutes per 450 g/1 lb.

Don't panic if the selection of fresh herbs is hard to find; use as many as you can and make up the missing amount with freshly chopped parsley.

▶ Wash the inside of the fish to remove all of the blood from behind the back bone. Lay the fish in a shallow dish with the herb sprigs, lemon juice, oil, white wine, fish stock and seasoning. Leave to marinate for up to 3 hours, or overnight if possible, turning the fish occasionally.

Place the fish in a steamer and strain the marinade into the saucepan below. Season the fish once more with salt and pepper. Cover with a tight fitting lid and steam for 20 minutes. (If your steamer will not accommodate a fish this size, use my suggestion under **Improvising** on page 9 and place the fish on a wire rack over a roasting tin containing the marinade; tightly seal with a large dome of foil.)

Transfer the fish to a warmed serving dish and keep hot. Reduce the steaming liquid by boiling rapidly until syrupy, lower the heat and whisk in the butter nut by nut until rich and creamy.

Stir in the chopped herbs. Taste and adjust seasoning if necessary. Pour the sauce over the fish or serve separately. Garnish with lemon wedges and sprigs of herbs.

1 kg/2 lb fresh whole fish, cleaned and descaled
sprigs of thyme, fennel, dill, chives and parsley for the marinade
juice of 1 lemon
2 tablespoons olive oil
300 ml/½ pint white wine
300 ml/½ pint fish stock
salt and freshly ground black pepper
50 g/2 oz butter cut into walnut-sized pieces
3 tablespoons chopped fresh herbs, for example, fennel, dill, chives and parsley
Garnish
lemon wedges
sprigs of herbs

GREY MULLET WITH PIQUANT TOMATO SAUCE

1 kg/2 lb grey mullet, cleaned and
  thoroughly scaled
salt and freshly ground black pepper
2 tablespoons white wine vinegar
2 tablespoons oil
parsley sprigs
Tomato sauce
1 tablespoon olive oil
2 shallots, finely chopped
1 large yellow pepper, deseeded and
  roughly chopped
1 (400-g/14-oz) can chopped
  tomatoes
1 teaspoon capers, rinsed
300 ml/½ pint fish stock
salt and freshly ground black pepper
Garnish
bunches of fennel leaves, dill,
  parsley or chives
1 tomato, peeled, deseeded and cut
  into julienne strips

If grey mullet is not available you may like to try this recipe with haddock fillets. It is also good with red mullet but because they are so much smaller you will have to remember to cut the cooking time by three-quarters and use two per person.

▶ Rinse the fish under cold water and remove any remaining blood from the backbone. Season well with salt and black pepper. Place the fish in a shallow dish with the vinegar, oil and parsley. Marinate for 3 hours or overnight if possible, turning occasionally.

Meanwhile make the sauce. Heat the oil in a saucepan and fry the shallot and pepper until cooked but not brown. Stir in the tomatoes, capers and stock. Season well with salt and pepper. Bring to the boil.

Discard the marinade, place the fish in a steamer and cover with a tight fitting lid. Steam over the sauce for 20 minutes. *Check the liquid level frequently and add boiling water if necessary.*

Remove the fish from the steamer, peel away the skin and keep warm. Blend the sauce in a liquidiser or food processor until smooth.

To serve, flood a warmed serving dish with half of the sauce. Lay the fish gently on top. Spoon on the remaining sauce.

Garnish with bunches of herbs and strips of tomato.

MONKFISH AND WILD MUSHROOM KEBABS

1 kg/2 lb monkfish, skinned and
  boned and cut into 32 bite-sized
  cubes
6 chanterelle mushrooms, rinsed
salt and freshly ground black pepper
juice of 1 lemon
1 tablespoon white wine vinegar
1 tablespoon olive oil
3 teaspoons green peppercorns, well
  rinsed
300 ml/½ pint fish stock
50 g/2 oz unsalted butter, cut into
  walnut-sized pieces
sprigs of chervil to garnish

Depending on seasonal availability, any variety of mushroom can be substituted for the chanterelles in the following recipe.

▶ Thread two cubes of fish on to each of four wooden skewers followed by a mushroom half, then continue the pattern until you have eight cubes of fish and three pieces of mushroom on each skewer. Season well with salt and black pepper. Mix the lemon juice, vinegar, oil and 1 teaspoon of the green peppercorns in a shallow dish. Lay the skewers in the marinade and marinate for 3 hours, turning occasionally.

Prepare the steamer by laying a flat sheet of foil over the base. Arrange the kebabs on top. Bring the marinade to the boil in a saucepan with the fish stock and the remaining 2 teaspoons green peppercorns. Cover with a tight fitting lid and steam the kebabs gently over the marinade and stock mixture for 15 minutes. *Check the liquid level frequently and add more boiling stock or water if necessary.*

Arrange the kebabs on warmed individual plates and keep hot. Reduce the stock by boiling rapidly until rich and syrupy. Over the heat, whisk in the butter, nut by nut, until the sauce is creamy and smooth. Spoon over the fish and garnish with sprigs of chervil. Serve at once.

STEAMED COD ON RED PEPPER SAUCE

It amazes me how some schools could ever turn this excellent fish into a shrivelled, tasteless lump – presumably 'the piece of cod which passeth all understanding!' Sweet red peppers and the delicate taste of marinated cod produces an elegant and juicy main course. When scorching the red peppers, the skin will peel off easily only if burnt completely black.

juice of 1 lemon
1 tablespoon olive oil
1 shallot, finely chopped
2 parsley sprigs
salt and freshly ground black pepper
4 (200–225-g/7–8-oz) cod steaks
2 red peppers
150 ml/¼ pint strong fish stock

▶ Mix the lemon juice, oil, shallot and parsley sprigs in a shallow dish. Season well with salt and pepper. Add the cod steaks, cover with the marinade and leave for up to 2 hours, turning occasionally.

Scorch the red peppers on the gas or electric ring until the skin is black all over. Peel away the burnt skin and rinse under clean water. Deseed and roughly chop one pepper and half of the second pepper, then cut the remaining half into thin strips and reserve for the garnish.

Place the fish stock and chopped peppers in a saucepan. Bring to the boil. Lay a piece of wet greaseproof paper in the steamer and arrange the cod steaks on top. Cover with a tight fitting lid. Steam over the stock for 8 minutes. Remove the cooked fish and keep warm. Blend the peppers and stock in a liquidiser until smooth. Taste and adjust the seasoning if necessary.

Arrange the red pepper sauce on four individual warmed plates. Top with the fish, sprinkle with thin strips of red pepper, and serve at once.

CONGER EEL WITH SWEETCORN DRESSING

I have to admit that conger eel is definitely a strong and acquired taste. It can be served either hot or cold, but I think cold is better.

1 corn on the cob
300 ml/½ pint fish stock
4 round cutlets of conger eel,
   skinned
salt and freshly ground black pepper
1 tablespoon chopped chives
1 tablespoon white wine vinegar
1 tablespoon olive oil
1 tablespoon lemon juice
mixed salad leaves, for example,
   iceberg, curly endive and radiccio
Garnish
4 rashers rindless streaky bacon,
   cooked and finely chopped
1 tablespoon chopped chives

▶ Remove the kernels from the sweetcorn and place both parts in a saucepan with the stock. Bring to the boil. Place the eel cutlets in a steamer, season with salt and pepper and sprinkle with the chives. Steam over the stock for 15–20 minutes. Remove, cover with damp greaseproof paper and allow to cool.

Remove the sweetcorn cob from the stock and discard. Stir in the vinegar. Taste and adjust seasoning if necessary. Blend in a liquidiser or food processor and sieve into a clean pan. Boil to reduce until syrupy. Allow the sauce to cool.

To serve, mix the oil and lemon together and season to taste. Toss the lettuce leaves lightly in the dressing. Arrange on four plates. Add the eel cutlets and spoon the sweetcorn sauce over the top. Sprinkle with chopped bacon and chives.

STEAMED SALMON TROUT

1.25 kg/2½ lb salmon trout, cleaned
225 g/8 oz rindless smoked lean back bacon, cut into strips
100 g/4 oz mushrooms, roughly chopped
salt and freshly ground black pepper
juice of 2 lemons
2 tablespoons olive oil
5 tablespoons white wine
1 large cos lettuce, separated into leaves and washed
600 ml/1 pint court bouillon (below)
sprigs of fresh herbs to garnish, for example, dill, fennel, chives, parsley
Hollandaise sauce
225 g/8 oz unsalted butter
2 egg yolks (size 3)
2 tablespoons lemon juice

The hollandaise sauce in this recipe can be flavoured with any herbs of your choice or simply left plain as below. Add a lemon slice for additional garnish, if liked.

▶ Wash the trout under running water. Check that there is no blood along the inside of the backbone, and if there is remove all of it to prevent a bitter-tasting end result. Mix the bacon and mushrooms together, season well, and use to stuff the cavity of the fish.

Lay the fish in a shallow dish containing the lemon juice, olive oil and white wine. Turning once or twice, marinate for 2–3 hours.

Steam the lettuce leaves for 30 seconds–1 minute, plunging them immediately afterwards into a bowl of iced water. Lay enough leaves side by side overlapping slightly to completely blanket the whole fish. Lift the salmon trout from the marinade and wrap in the lettuce leaves, seasoning well as you go.

Bring the remaining marinade to the boil with the court bouillon. Place the lettuce parcel in a steamer above the pan. Cover well and steam for 20 minutes.

Meanwhile make the hollandaise sauce. Melt the butter in a saucepan until it bubbles. Blend the egg yolks with the lemon juice in a liquidiser or food processor, and season well with salt and pepper. Gradually pour in the butter in a thin stream. When all of the butter has been incorporated, turn off the machine immediately. Pour the sauce into a bowl and place it on top of a pan of hot water until it has warmed through thoroughly.

Lay the fish parcel on a warmed serving dish sprinkled with sprigs of fresh herbs and serve the sauce separately.

COURT BOUILLON

1.15 litres/2 pints water
150 ml/¼ pint vinegar
1 carrot, washed and sliced
1 small onion, peeled and studded with a clove
1 celery stick, sliced
8 peppercorns · 2 bay leaves
3 parsley stalks · salt

Court Bouillon is the traditional liquid in which to poach fish, but also adds flavour when used as a base for steaming fish.

▶ Bring all of the ingredients to the boil and salt lightly. Cover and simmer for 20 minutes. Strain before using.

From the top: *Plaits of Salmon and Turbot (page 16);*
Steamed Salmon Trout

PLAIT OF SALMON & TURBOT

1.5 kg/3 lb salmon or trout fillets,
  skinned
675 g/1½ lb turbot or plaice fillets,
  skinned
1.15 litres/2 pints court bouillon
Chive hollandaise
225 g/8 oz unsalted butter
3 egg yolks
2 tablespoons lemon juice
salt and freshly ground black pepper
2 tablespoons chopped chives
dill sprigs or chopped chives to
  garnish

I have adapted this from my college days when Prue Leith gave us fish to plait. I can assure you that it looks excellent, is not difficult to do, and is an expensive treat for those that eat it. Use salmon trout and plaice for a cheaper alternative.

▶ Cut the salmon into eight (15-cm/6-in × 1-cm/½-in × 1-cm/½-in) strips. Cut the turbot into four identical strips. Plait the fish using two pink strips and one white. Place a layer of wet greaseproof paper in a steamer and lay the plaits neatly on top. Bring the court bouillon to the boil. Cover the fish with a tight fitting lid and steam over the court bouillon for 10 minutes or until the fish is just firm.

  Five minutes before serving, make the chive hollandaise. Melt the butter in a saucepan. Blend the egg yolks with the lemon juice, salt and pepper in a liquidiser or food processor. Gradually pour in the butter in a thin stream. When all the butter has been incorporated, turn off the machine immediately. Stir in the chives, pour the sauce into a suitable bowl and put over hot water until required.

  To serve, flood four individual plates with chive hollandaise. Gently lay a fish plait on each. Garnish with chives and eat immediately.

TARRAGON TURBOT

4 (175-g/6-oz) turbot steaks
salt and freshly ground black pepper
juice of 1 lime
sprigs of tarragon
300 ml/½ pint fish stock
150 ml/¼ pint double cream
1 carrot, cut into julienne strips
2 celery sticks, cut into julienne
  strips
2 teaspoons chopped fresh tarragon
sprigs of tarragon to garnish

I have used tarragon here but any delicate aromatic herb, such as dill or fennel leaves, is equally as good.

▶ Season the fish with salt and black pepper. Lay in a shallow dish with the lime juice and tarragon sprigs. Marinate for about 2 hours, turning occasionally. Place the fish stock and cream in the base of the steamer. Bring to the boil. Lay a wet piece of greaseproof paper in the top compartment.

  Arrange the fish and vegetables on top. Spoon on any remaining marinade. Cover with a tightly fitting lid. Steam for 7 minutes. Remove the turbot and vegetables and put to one side to keep warm. Boil the stock to reduce to the consistency of single cream. Stir in the chopped tarragon. Taste and adjust seasoning if necessary.

  Flood four warmed plates with the sauce. Arrange the turbot and vegetables on top. Garnish with sprigs of tarragon.

  Serve immediately.

STUFFED FILLETS OF PLAICE

For this recipe you can use either Dover or lemon sole instead of plaice unless you want to save a few pennies, in which case plaice is perfectly good.

▶ Lay the fillets flat in a shallow dish with the oil and vinegar. Roughly chop two of the basil leaves and sprinkle over the fish. Season well with salt and pepper and marinate for up to 2 hours.

Meanwhile place the courgette in a colander and sprinkle with salt. Leave for 30 minutes. Rinse well under running cold water to remove all the salt and pat dry with absorbent kitchen paper. Mix together a quarter of the tomato and courgette slices in a bowl and season well.

Remove the fillets from the marinade and gently pat dry. Place one teaspoon of the tomato and courgette mixture and 1 basil leaf at one end of each fillet. Season well. Roll up tightly and place side by side in the steamer. Bring the court bouillon to the boil. Cover the plaice with a tight fitting lid and steam over the court bouillon for 6–8 minutes.

Meanwhile, heat the remaining courgette and tomato slices in a saucepan, but do not allow to stew. Check seasonings. Divide the mixture between four individual plates. Arrange the stuffed plaice on top. Spoon on a little melted butter and lemon juice. Garnish with basil sprigs.

Eat at once.

4 fresh plaice, filleted in halves and skinned
2 tablespoons olive oil
1 tablespoon white wine vinegar
10 small basil leaves
salt and freshly ground black pepper
350 g/12 oz courgettes, finely sliced
450 g/1 lb ripe tomatoes, peeled, deseeded and finely sliced
600 ml/1 pint court bouillon
50 g/2 oz melted butter
juice of 2 lemons
sprigs of basil to garnish

MIDSUMMER FANTASIE

Use fresh asparagus if possible for this delightful and easy summer dish that tastes as colourful as it looks.

▶ Cut the cucumber and salmon into julienne strips. Season the asparagus with salt and pepper and lemon juice. Steam the asparagus over boiling water for 3 minutes.

Meanwhile make the dressing. Place the mustard, sugar, oil, fromage frais or quark, dill and seasoning to taste in a screw-topped jar, shake thoroughly, taste and adjust seasoning if necessary.

Arrange the cooked asparagus on four individual plates, and sprinkle on the cucumber and salmon. Garnish with sprigs of dill. Serve with mustard dressing.

225 g/8 oz cucumber
100 g/4 oz sliced smoked salmon
8 white asparagus stalks, peeled
20 small green asparagus stalks, peeled
salt and freshly ground black pepper
juice of 1 lemon
1 tablespoon Dijon mustard
2 tablespoons granulated sugar
6 tablespoons olive oil
2 tablespoons fromage frais or quark
1 tablespoon chopped fresh dill
sprigs of dill to garnish

SQUID SALAD WITH CITRUS HERB DRESSING

675 g/1½ lb prepared squid
16 small green asparagus tips
75 g/3 oz mangetout, topped and
    tailed
juice of 1 lemon
salt and freshly ground black pepper
small head of radiccio, separated
    into leaves and washed
Dressing
4 tablespoons olive oil
3 tablespoons lemon vinegar
50 g/2 oz fromage frais or quark
1 tablespoon finely chopped fresh
    herbs, for example, dill, chervil,
    parsley
sprigs of dill and chervil to garnish
    (optional)

The quality of squid whether fresh or frozen is generally very good. Try when possible to obtain small squid as they can be cooked in just a few minutes and are sweet and tender.

▶ Slice the squid into thin rings. Lay a piece of wet greaseproof paper in the steamer. Arrange the asparagus, mangetout and squid on top. Sprinkle over the lemon juice and season well with salt and black pepper. Cover and steam over boiling water for 3 minutes.

Meanwhile mix all the dressing ingredients in a screw-topped jar. Season well with salt and pepper. Arrange the radiccio leaves on a serving dish. Toss the warm food in the dressing and pile on to the radiccio leaves. Garnish with sprigs of dill and chervil, if liked.

COLOURFUL MUSSELS

This recipe is a fun variation of the famous moules marinire. A mixture of fresh herbs adds immeasurably to the appearance and taste of the dish, so use any herbs that you can get hold of, except perhaps mint as it is slightly overpowering. Then choose a colourful selection of seasonal vegetables, or simply follow my recipe!

▶ Discard any open mussels or those that do not shut when firmly tapped. Melt the butter in the base of a large saucepan. Gently fry the shallot, garlic and fennel until cooked but not brown. Add the wine and simmer for 5 minutes. Put the mussels in the pan, and sprinkle with the herbs and vegetable strips. Season with salt and freshly ground black pepper. Cover with a tightly fitting lid. Steam the mussels for 3–5 minutes, shaking the pan from time to time.

Discard any unopened shellfish. Transfer the mussels and vegetable strips to a warmed serving dish and keep hot. Blend the fennel and garlic mixture in a liquidiser, adding the fromage frais. Taste and adjust seasoning if necessary. Pour the sauce over the mussels and garnish with fennel leaves.

2 kg/4¼ lb mussels, scrubbed and beard removed
25 g/1oz butter
2 shallots, very finely chopped
3 cloves garlic, crushed
bulb of fennel, very finely chopped
150 ml/¼ pint white wine
1 tablespoon fennel leaves
1 tablespoon chopped parsley
½ tablespoon chopped chives
1 carrot, cut into julienne strips
1 leek, trimmed washed and cut into julienne strips
1 parsnip, peeled and cut into julienne strips
salt and freshly ground black pepper
50 g/2 oz fromage frais
fennel leaves to garnish

SCALLOP BROCHETTE

16 prepared large scallops, fresh if
   possible
juice of 2 limes
2 teaspoons chopped fresh tarragon
salt and freshly ground black pepper
6 tablespoons olive oil
1 mango, peeled, stoned and diced
300 ml/½ pint white wine
4 sprigs tarragon
2 bay leaves
150 ml/¼ pint water
Garnish
sprigs of tarragon
mango slices (optional)
lime slices (optional)

Scallops are delicately flavoured shellfish that require very little cooking time and respond best to gentle steaming. To make the brochette into a main course or light lunch, simply double the quantities and serve on a bed of saffron rice. The rice can be cooked in the saucepan below whilst the kebabs are gently steaming above.

▶ Cut the white flesh of the scallop into quarters. Keep the pink coral whole. Marinate in the lime juice and tarragon, seasoned well with salt and pepper, for up to 2 hours.

Skewer eight scallop quarters and two corals on each of eight wooden kebab sticks, retaining the marinade for the dressing. Make a dressing by mixing the oil, marinade and mango in a screw-topped jar, shake well and season to taste.

Put the wine, sprigs of tarragon, bay leaves and water into a saucepan. Place the kebabs in a steamer above the pan, cover with a tight fitting lid and cook for 3 minutes.

Arrange two kebabs on each of four plates, spoon on plenty of lime and mango dressing. Garnish with sprigs of tarragon and serve immediately.

PEPPERED SCALLOPS

2 tablespoons sesame oil
juice of one lemon
15 g/½ oz fresh root ginger, peeled
   and grated
1 large clove of garlic, crushed
salt and freshly ground black pepper
16 prepared large scallops, fresh
Dressing
3 tablespoons sesame oil
1 tablespoon lemon juice
1 shallot, finely chopped
1 tablespoon soy sauce
100 g/4 oz unsalted butter cut into
   walnut-sized pieces
1 tablespoon sesame seeds to
   garnish
Sauce
1 red pepper
1 green pepper
1 yellow pepper
300 ml/½ pint fish stock

This dish is beautiful to look at and a delight to eat. Take care not to cut the pink coral as it will fall apart during cooking. Never let scallops overcook, so keep an eye on the time.

▶ Mix together the oil, lemon juice, ginger and garlic, season well with freshly ground pepper and salt. Remove the pink coral whole from the scallop shell. Cut the white flesh in two. Marinate in the oil and lemon mixture for up to 2 hours.

Meanwhile make the dressing. Place all ingredients in a screw-topped jar and shake well. Taste and adjust seasonings if necessary.

Put the stock and any remaining marinade in the base of the steamer. Arrange the mixed peppers in the steaming compartment with the scallops on top. Cover with a tightly fitting lid and cook for 3 minutes. Remove the scallops, toss in the dressing and keep warm. Add the peppers to the stock. Boil to reduce until syrupy. Reduce the heat and whisk in the butter, nut by nut until you have a creamy sauce. Check seasoning.

Flood four individual plates with mixed pepper sauce. Arrange the scallops on top and sprinkle with sesame seeds.

SHELLFISH RAGOÛT

Ragoût simply means a stew of meat or fish and vegetables. I have rather selfishly chosen the variety of shellfish which I enjoy the most and have used vegetables that are most varied in texture and brightly coloured. As long as you follow the basic method you could use any of your favourite seafood and vegetables.

▶ If the scampi or prawns are raw, steam for 5 minutes over the fish stock, and leave to cool slightly. Remove the shells from the scampi, roughly chop and add the shells to the fish stock, (leave the scampi to one side). Simmer for 10 minutes then discard the shells.

Otherwise place the carrots, radishes and mangetout in the steamer, cover with a tight fitting lid and steam over the fish stock for 3 minutes. Meanwhile cut the scampi and scallops in half, taking care to leave the coral whole. Place all the shellfish in the steamer with the vegetables. Sprinkle with lemon juice and dill sprigs. Season well with salt and pepper. Steam for 3–5 minutes. Remove, set aside and keep warm.

Reduce the stock by half by boiling rapidly. Add the watercress and fromage frais, then blend the sauce in a liquidiser or food processor. Taste and adjust seasoning if necessary.

Pile the shellfish on a bed of sauce, garnish with dill and watercress. Serve immediately.

12 scampi or Mediterranean prawns alive if possible, or frozen
300 ml/½ pint strong fish stock
12 baby new carrots
8 radishes, topped and tailed
75 g/3 oz mangetout, topped and tailed
4 prepared large scallops, fresh if possible or 8 Queen scallops
350 g/12 oz mussels, scrubbed and beard removed
225 g/8 oz fresh clams, scrubbed
juice of 1 lemon
2 sprigs dill
salt and freshly ground black pepper
½ bunch of watercress
75 g/3 oz fromage frais
Garnish
dill sprigs
watercress sprigs

FRESH LOBSTER SALAD

▶ Bring a large saucepan of water to the boil then let it go cold; this removes the dissolved oxygen from the water and effectively anaesthetises the lobsters before they are steamed.

Bring a second large saucepan of water to the boil. Place the live lobsters in the cool water for 3 minutes, then put them straight into a steamer and steam over the boiling water for 15 minutes. Remove the lobsters and leave them to cool down.

Melt the butter in a pan, and gently fry the carrot and shallot until soft but not brown. Add the stock and herbs, and season well. Simmer for 10–15 minutes. Blend the sauce in a liquidiser, and add the vinegar. When the lobsters are slightly cooler, remove the tails and cut through the shell underneath with scissors. Carefully open out the shells and remove the tail meat in one piece. Remove and carefully crack the claws, lift out the meat, discarding the cartilage. Cut the tail meat into thin medallions and cut the claws in half.

Mix together the oil and 2 tablespoons of the lemon juice. Season well with salt and pepper. Toss the chicory, endive and lettuce leaves in the dressing. Peel and slice the avocados and brush with a little lemon juice. Pour the carrot coulis on to four individual plates. Arrange the leaves, lobster and avocado on each plate. Serve at once, or cover and chill in the refrigerator.

2 (450-g/1-lb) live female lobsters
25 g/1 oz butter
575 g/1¼ lb carrots, grated
2 shallots, finely chopped
300 ml/½ pint vegetable stock
2–3 sprigs dill
2–3 sprigs thyme
1 tablespoon chopped chives
salt and freshly ground black pepper
1 tablespoon red wine vinegar
3 tablespoons olive oil
juice of 1 lemon
head of chicory, separated into leaves and washed
1 small curly endive, separated into leaves and washed
1 lettuce heart, separated into leaves and washed
2 avocados

MILLIONAIRE'S MOUSSE

450 g/1 lb sole, filleted, skinned and roughly chopped
450 g/1 lb turbot, filleted, skinned and roughly chopped
3 egg whites
salt and freshly ground black pepper
300 ml/½ pint double cream
1 cooked lobster tail, shelled, meat cubed, or 75 g/3 oz peeled cooked prawns, or 75 g/3 oz peeled cooked scampi
juice of ½ lemon
15 g/½ oz fresh root ginger, peeled and grated
3 red peppers, scorched and peeled
150 ml/¼ pint strong fish stock
Garnish
finely chopped red pepper
coriander leaves

You are sure to impress your guests with the exquisite flavour combinations of this recipe. However if you're not quite a millionaire, you can replace the lobster with scampi or prawns.
For this one you will also need to have access to a food processor.

▶ Lightly oil a 1-litre/1¾-pint ring mould. Leave upside down on absorbent kitchen paper to drain. Place the fish in a food processor and blend until smooth. Add the egg whites and blend until absolutely smooth. Season very well with salt and black pepper. With the machine running, pour in the cream. Do not process for more than 20 seconds. Check seasoning again and pour into the ring mould. Chill for 30 minutes.

Meanwhile marinate the lobster, prawns or scampi in the lemon juice and ginger. Chill. Place the peppers and fish stock in a saucepan. Cover the ring mould with foil or greaseproof paper and place in the steamer, cover with a tight fitting lid and steam over the peppers and stock for 15 minutes. Remove the ring mould from the steamer and keep warm. Blend the peppers and stock in a liquidiser or food processor until smooth. Sieve twice until thoroughly smooth.

To serve, flood a warm serving plate with the pepper sauce. Heat the lobster in a pan. Turn the fish ring out on to the pool of sauce. Fill the hole with the gingered lobster. Sprinkle with chopped red pepper and coriander leaves. Serve immediately.

THE GREEN JACKETS

25 g/1 oz butter, melted
225 g/8 oz spinach
1 kg/2 lb smoked haddock fillets, skinned and any bones removed
4 egg whites
75 g/3 oz Gruyère cheese, grated
salt and freshly ground black pepper
pinch of cayenne
pinch of grated nutmeg
300 ml/½ pint double cream
melba toast to serve

Served with steamed, colourful vegetables, this smoked fish mousse wrapped in a light spinach coat would make a substantial main course, but on its own is a perfect start to any meal. Any smoked fish could be used instead of haddock without affecting the pretty primrose colour, and you could just as easily use lettuce instead of spinach.

▶ Brush the inside of four ramekins with melted butter. Drain upside down on absorbent kitchen paper. Wash the spinach and discard any thick stalks. Steam the spinach leaves for 15 seconds and use them to line the ramekins, bringing them up and over the sides of the dishes.

Blend the fish in a liquidiser until smooth, add the egg whites and cheese. When completely smooth, season well with salt, pepper, cayenne and nutmeg. With the machine running, pour in the cream. Do not blend for more than 20 seconds.

Divide the mixture between the four ramekins. Bring any overlapping spinach on top of the mousse. Cover the ramekins in foil. Half-fill a saucepan with water, bring to the boil and place the mousses in the steamer. Cover with a tight fitting lid and steam over the boiling water for 20 minutes.

Turn out into four individual plates and serve hot or cold with melba toast.

POULTRY & GAME BIRDS

Poultry is now eaten more regularly than meat. Not only is it a valuable source of protein, vitamins and minerals, but it is also easy to digest. The difference in colour between white poultry such as chicken and turkey, and dark such as game, duck and goose, does not affect the quality of nutrients. Most of the saturated fat on domestic birds is on or around the skin and can be removed before eating. Game birds are less rich in fat than their domestic cousins and are renowned for drying out during cooking. Steaming is the answer to this problem: it is a cooking method that guarantees a succulent and juicy result for all poultry and game, and it also seals in all the goodness and taste. Chicken is the most popular bird because of its mild, pleasant flavour, versatility and value for money. When buying any fresh poultry or game bird, check that the breastbone is flexible, and that the breast is plump.

Chicken Pinwheels (page 24)

CHICKEN PINWHEELS

4 boneless chicken breasts
salt and freshly ground black pepper
leaves from sprig of thyme
2 tablespoons chopped chives
juice of 1 lemon
2 cloves garlic, crushed
100 g/4 oz chicken livers, trimmed
    and washed
4 knobs butter
Stilton Sauce
175 g/6 oz blue brie, rind removed
300 ml/$\frac{1}{2}$ pint fromage frais
150 ml/$\frac{1}{4}$ pint soured cream
1$\frac{1}{2}$ tablespoons red wine vinegar
$\frac{1}{2}$ yellow pepper, very finely chopped
$\frac{1}{2}$ red pepper, very finely chopped
salt and freshly ground black pepper
Garnish
chives
coriander sprigs

On a hot summer's day, all your body needs is something cool and light. Serve with a selection of interesting salads.
    This makes an ideal and unusual picnic treat.

▶ Place each chicken breast between two pieces of greaseproof paper. Beat to flatten slightly with a rolling pin. Season the breasts with salt and pepper. Sprinkle each with thyme leaves, chives, lemon juice and garlic. Spread about 25 g/1 oz of chicken livers on each breast, leaving a gap of about 1 cm/$\frac{1}{2}$ in around the perimeter of the chicken breast. Roll up and spread the outsides with a knob of butter, then wrap the breasts tightly in foil. Steam over boiling water for 40 minutes. Leave until completely cold.

To make the sauce, blend the blue brie, fromage frais, soured cream and vinegar in a food processor or liquidiser. Stir in half of the chopped peppers, and season well with salt and pepper. Unwrap the chicken rolls and add any chicken juices to the sauce, stirring well.

Pour the sauce on to four individual plates. Slice the chicken rolls and arrange on the sauce. Sprinkle on the remaining peppers. Garnish with chives and coriander sprigs.

CHICKEN WITH GARLIC AND ROOT VEGETABLES

1 (1.75-kg/4-lb) oven-ready roasting
    chicken with giblets
1 small onion, roughly chopped
1 teaspoon olive oil
2 bay leaves
6 peppercorns
300 ml/$\frac{1}{2}$ pint dry white wine
600 ml/1 pint water
1 tablespoon vegetable peelings
grated rind and juice of 1 lemon
sprigs of tarragon and chervil
salt and freshly ground black pepper
20 cloves of garlic, *not* peeled
8 baby carrots
4 small parsnips, peeled
8 baby leeks, trimmed
2 tablespoons chopped fresh herbs,
    for example, tarragon, chervil,
    parsley, to garnish

Twenty cloves of garlic is not a misprint and I can assure you I am not mad! When garlic is cooked, the flavour is subtle and when puréed it is a useful non-fat thickener for sauces. If a 4-lb chicken isn't going to fit into your steamer however hard you push, try and buy two double-poussin, split the recipe in half and cook in two steamers.

▶ Fry the giblets and onion in the oil until golden brown. Add the bay leaves, peppercorns, wine, water and vegetable peelings. Bring to the boil and simmer for 20 minutes, in order to make a stock. Meanwhile, wipe the chicken, pour on the lemon juice, sprinkle inside and outside with the grated rind and herbs. Season very well with salt and black pepper.

Strain the stock into the base of the steamer. Bring to the boil. Sit the chicken on the unpeeled garlic cloves in the steamer. Cover with a tight fitting lid and steam for 45 minutes. *Check the liquid level frequently and add more boiling stock or water if necessary.*

Season the vegetables with salt and pepper and place in the steamer with the chicken, cover and continue to cook for 15 minutes.

Push the garlic cloves through a sieve into the stock. Discard the skins, stir well, taste and adjust seasoning if necessary. If the stock is already the thickness of single cream then pour over the chicken. If not, boil to reduce until it is the right thickness. Sprinkle the bird with herbs and serve at once.

SUPRÊME OF CHICKEN ON A WARM SALAD OF CHICORY

Suprême literally means the best part of the bird: in other words the breast. You could use any piece of boneless poultry for this recipe, but do try hard to get the walnut oil – you won't regret it!

▶ Season the chicken breasts with salt and pepper. Lay them in a shallow dish with the oil, lemon juice, tarragon, walnut and onion. Leave to marinate for 2 hours.

Cut four 35-cm/14-in-square sheets of foil. Place a chicken breast on each and spoon on equal amounts of marinade. Fold up the edges of the foil to seal the parcels completely. Steam over boiling water for 15 minutes.

Meanwhile, wash and dry the lettuce, wash the chicory and separate it into leaves; shake the dressing ingredients together in a screw-topped jar, and arrange the salad leaves on four plates. Pour the contents of a parcel on each plate and spoon on the extra dressing. Garnish with walnuts and tarragon sprigs.

4 chicken breasts, skinned, wingbone cleaned but all other bones removed
salt and freshly ground pepper
4 tablespoons walnut oil
juice of 1 lemon
sprigs of tarragon
50 g/2 oz walnuts, finely chopped
3 red or small white onions, sliced
head of oak leaf lettuce
head of chicory
Dressing
4 tablespoons walnut oil
2 tablespoons tarragon vinegar
1 teaspoon prepared mustard
1 tablespoon chopped walnuts
salt and freshly ground black pepper
Garnish
chopped walnuts
sprigs of tarragon

CHICKEN HOT POT

For winter warmth there is nothing better. Use heaps of any vegetable you can get your hands on.

▶ Heat the oil in a heavy-based pan. Season the chicken with salt, pepper and lemon juice. Fry the chicken on both sides until golden brown. Place in a heatproof mixing bowl that will fit inside your largest saucepan or steamer.

Fry the vegetables for 2 minutes until golden brown. Spoon them over the chicken. Pour the stock, wine and port into the frying pan. Bring to the boil, scraping the sediment from the base of the pan. Pour over the chicken. Add the herbs. Season well with salt and freshly ground black pepper. Cover the bowl with foil or greaseproof paper and tie down with string.

Place in saucepan of boiling water with a tight fitting lid, or in a steamer, and steam for 1½ hours. *Check the liquid level frequently and add more boiling water if necessary.*

Remove the foil or paper. Pour the liquid from the chicken into a small saucepan. Arrange the meat and vegetables in a warmed serving dish and keep warm. Boil the stock to reduce to a syrupy consistency. Spoon over the meat and garnish with sprigs of herbs.

2 tablespoons olive oil
1 (1.75-kg/4-lb) chicken, jointed into 8 pieces
salt and freshly ground black pepper
juice of 1 lemon
225 g/8 oz Jerusalem artichokes, peeled and halved
225 g/8 oz Brussels sprouts, trimmed
225 g/8 oz carrots, cut into bite-sized pieces
225 g/8 oz swede, peeled and cut into bite-sized pieces
100 g/4 oz small turnips, peeled and quartered
100 g/4 oz parsnips, peeled and cut into bite-sized pieces
300 ml/½ pint chicken stock
300 ml/½ pint red wine
50 ml/2 fl oz port
large bunch of herbs, for example, thyme, parsley, tarragon
sprigs of herbs, for example, thyme, parsley, tarragon, to garnish

LEMON-SCENTED POUSSIN

4 (350-g/12-oz) poussin, washed and
  dried
grated rind and juice of 1 lemon
150 ml/¼ pint dry white wine
sprigs of thyme, marjoram and
  oregano for the marinade
salt and freshly ground black pepper
2 tablespoons olive oil
½ red cabbage, cut into julienne
  strips
½ white cabbage, cut into julienne
  strips
4 tablespoons chopped fresh thyme,
  marjoram and oregano
150 ml/¼ pint double cream
600 ml/1 pint chicken stock
sprig of lemon grass
sprigs or chopped fresh mixed herbs
  to garnish

Try to get hold of lemon grass but if that is impossible use the grated rind of an extra lemon.

▶ Place the poussin in a dish with the lemon rind and juice, white wine and herbs. Season well with salt and pepper. Marinate for up to 2 hours. Remove from the marinade and dry well. Heat the oil in a heavy-based pan. Fry the poussin over high heat until golden brown on all sides.

Spread the red and white cabbage over the base of the steamer. Top with the four poussin. Season well with salt and pepper. Spoon over the chopped fresh herbs. Pour the remaining marinade into the saucepan with the double cream, chicken stock and lemon grass. Cover with a tight fitting lid and steam over the stock for 40–45 minutes. *Check the liquid level frequently and add more boiling stock or water if necessary.*

Arrange each poussin on a bed of mixed cabbage and keep warm. Remove the lemon grass and reduce the stock until rich and creamy. Pour over the poussin, garnish with sprigs of herbs.

Serve immediately.

CHICKEN IN LETTUCE

600 ml/1 pint chicken stock
300 ml/½ pint dry cider
8 large cos lettuce leaves, washed
4 chicken breasts, skinned
50 g/2 oz butter, softened
2 cloves garlic, crushed
salt and freshly ground black pepper
2 large carrots, cut into matchsticks
2 celery sticks, cut into matchsticks
50 g/2 oz smoked ham, cut into
  strips
juice of 1 lemon
100 g/4 oz unsalted butter, cut into
  walnut-sized pieces
fennel to garnish

Steamed chicken is succulent and juicy. This recipe will give you guaranteed enjoyment.

Do make sure that you check the liquid level during steaming and you should add boiling cider if the level is too low.

▶ Bring the chicken stock and cider to the boil in the base of the steamer. Place the lettuce leaves in a steamer and steam over the stock and cider for 20 seconds or until just limp. Dry on absorbent kitchen paper.

With a knife, spread the chicken breasts with the softened butter and garlic and season both sides well with salt and black pepper. Lay down the lettuce leaves in pairs, overlapping slightly. Lay each chicken breast at the stalk end of the leaves. Divide three-quarters of the vegetables and all of the ham between the four breasts and spoon on top of each chicken breast.

Blanch the remaining vegetables, drain, then put to one side for the garnish. Squeeze the lemon juice over the chicken, fold the leaves over the mixture and lay the chicken side down in the steaming compartment. Cover and steam for 20 mins. *Check the liquid level frequently and add more boiling cider if necessary.*

When cooked, remove the chicken parcels and keep warm. Reduce the stock until syrupy by boiling rapidly. Lower heat and whisk in the butter, nut by nut until you have a smooth, creamy sauce. Check seasoning.

Flood four individual plates with cider sauce, then lay the chicken parcels on top. Sprinkle with remaining vegetables and garnish with fennel.

POUSSIN WITH SPICY HOT SAUCE

2 tablespoons walnut oil (olive oil will do)
4 (350-g/12-oz) poussin
salt and freshly ground black pepper
juice of 1 lemon
2 bunches of spring onions, trimmed and finely chopped
2 chillies, deseeded and finely chopped
pinch of cayenne
300 ml/½ pint chicken stock
large bunch of watercress, washed and large stalks removed
50 g/2 oz fromage frais
watercress sprigs to garnish

This interesting combination of flavours proved to be an enormous success when served at one of my recipe testing parties. If you are nervous of the power of chillies then reduce the quantity below by half. It was the perfect heat for me!

▶ Heat the oil in a heavy-based pan. Season the birds with salt, pepper and lemon juice. Fry over a high heat until golden brown on all sides. Remove from the pan and set aside. Fry the spring onions and chilli in the same pan with the cayenne and a little salt for 3 minutes. Lay a piece of wet greaseproof paper in the steamer. Spread the spring onion mixture on top. Arrange the poussin in the spring onions.

Pour the chicken stock into the frying pan. Bring to the boil, scraping the sediment from the base of the pan. Pour into the saucepan. Cover the poussin with a tight fitting lid and steam over the stock for 20 minutes. Add three-quarters of the watercress and continue to cook for 10 minutes. *Check liquid level frequently and add more stock or boiling water if necessary.*

Remove the poussin to one side and keep warm. Add the spring onion and chilli mixture and the remaining watercress to the stock. Blend in a liquidiser until smooth. Add the fromage frais. Taste and adjust seasoning if necessary.

Flood four warmed plates with the watercress sauce. Top with the poussin and garnish with watercress sprigs.

TURKEY FRICASSÉE ON ANGEL HAIR PASTA

1 kg/2 lb boneless turkey pieces, skinned
1 tablespoon olive oil
2 cloves garlic, crushed
2 leeks, trimmed, washed and finely sliced
225 g/8 oz cap mushrooms, wiped and stalks trimmed
1 (400-g/14-oz) can chopped tomatoes in natural juice
50 ml/2 fl oz red wine vinegar
50 ml/2 fl oz red wine
2 tablespoons chopped fresh basil
salt and freshly ground black pepper
450 g/1 lb Angel Hair pasta (page 96)
1 tablespoon olive oil
basil leaves to garnish

▶ Cut the turkey into bite-sized pieces. Heat the oil in a pan. Fry the turkey until golden brown on all sides. Transfer to a pudding basin. Gently fry the garlic and leeks in the same pan until cooked but not brown. Add the mushrooms, tomatoes, vinegar, wine and 1 tablespoon of the basil. Season very well with salt and freshly ground black pepper. Bring to the boil and pour the sauce over the turkey. Cover with foil and place in the steamer or saucepan half-filled with boiling water. Cover with a tight fitting lid and steam for 20 minutes.

To make Angel Hair Pasta, turn to the recipe on page 96. Two minutes before serving the fricassée, put the pasta and oil in with the boiling water. Be careful not to overcook the pasta.

Drain the pasta, season and stir in the remaining chopped basil. Divide between four warmed plates. Spoon on the turkey and sauce. Garnish with basil leaves. Serve at once.

TURKEY KEBABS WITH FRESH ONION MARMALADE

I love the combination of Chinese marinated turkey with this sharp onion sauce. It is quick to prepare and cook and its exquisite combination of flavours should appeal to everyone.

▶ Thread the turkey and red onion quarters on to four kebab skewers. Lay in a shallow dish with the soy sauce, sherry, ginger and garlic. Leave to marinate for 2 hours, turning occasionally. Pour the marinade and stock into the base of the steamer. Stir in the onions. Bring to the boil. Lay a piece of wet greaseproof paper in the top compartment. Arrange the kebabs on top. Season well with salt and freshly ground black pepper. Cover with a tightly fitting lid and steam over the stock for 15–20 minutes. *Check the liquid level frequently, and add more boiling stock or water if necessary.*

Remove the kebabs to one side and keep warm. Stir the vinegar and honey into the onion mixture. Boil to reduce until syrupy. Taste to check seasoning, adjust if necessary.

Arrange the kebabs on warmed plates. Spoon over the sauce and garnish with chopped peppers and coriander leaves.

1 kg/2 lb boneless turkey, cut into bite-sized pieces
4 red onions, quartered
2 tablespoons light soy sauce
2 tablespoons dry sherry
15 g/$\frac{1}{2}$ oz fresh root ginger, peeled and finely chopped
2 cloves garlic, crushed
450 ml/$\frac{3}{4}$ pint chicken stock
675 g/1$\frac{1}{2}$ lb red or white onions, finely sliced
salt and freshly ground black pepper
2 tablespoons red wine vinegar
2 tablespoons clear honey
Garnish
$\frac{1}{4}$ yellow pepper, deseeded and finely chopped
$\frac{1}{4}$ green pepper, deseeded and finely chopped
sprigs of coriander

GINGERED DUCK BREASTS

Duck with orange is a popular and successful combination of flavours. The addition of ginger will both intrigue and delight your guests. Use wild duck if you can, but domestic will do perfectly well.

▶ Pare the rind of one of the oranges and cut into needleshreds, blanch for 20 seconds and set to one side. Lay the duck breasts in a dish with the juice of two oranges, the ginger, sherry, vinegar and half of the prepared needleshreds. Season well with salt and pepper. Marinate for up to 2 hours.

Peel the remaining orange, removing all of the pith, and cut into segments retaining the juice. Bring the stock and all of the marinade to the boil, in a saucepan, stirring in the segments and juice.

Lay a piece of wet greaseproof paper in the steamer and arrange the duck breasts on top. Cover with a tight fitting lid and steam over the stock for 20 minutes. *Check the liquid level frequently and add more boiling stock or water if necessary.* Remove the duck and keep warm whilst finishing the sauce.

Blend the stock in a liquidiser and rub through a sieve. Reduce by boiling rapidly until rich and syrupy. Lower the heat, whisk in the butter nut by nut until you have a rich creamy sauce. Taste and adjust seasoning if necessary.

Arrange the duck on warmed plates and pour over the sauce. Garnish with remaining needleshreds and parsley.

3 oranges
4 duck breasts, skinned
15 g/$\frac{1}{2}$ oz root ginger, peeled and finely chopped
2 tablespoons sherry
1 tablespoon red wine vinegar
salt and freshly ground black pepper
450 ml/$\frac{3}{4}$ pints chicken or duck stock
100 g/4 oz unsalted butter, cut into walnut-sized pieces
Garnish
needleshreds of orange rind
flat-leaf parsley

STEAMED WILD DUCK LIVERS

450 g/1 lb duck livers, washed and
    trimmed
50 ml/2 fl oz milk
300 ml/½ pint duck or chicken stock
3 spring onions, trimmed and sliced
1 carrot, finely diced
salt and freshly ground black pepper
1 tablespoon honey
2 teaspoons red wine vinegar
small head of radiccio, washed and
    cut into separate leaves
bunch of watercress
Garnish
50 g/2 oz smoked ham, cut into
    strips (optional)
finely chopped spring onion tips
    (optional)

*Wild duck livers are indescribably delicious but not always easy to get hold of.
Use normal duck livers if necessary; you won't be too disappointed!*
    *Duck liver is the healthiest part of the bird to eat, as it is packed with vitamins
and minerals. It should be served on a bed of bitter leaves.*

▶ Soak the livers in the milk for 30 minutes. Discard the milk, rinse the livers
and pat dry. Bring the stock to the boil in a saucepan. Lay a sheet of wet
greaseproof paper in the steamer. Place the livers, spring onion and carrot on
top. Season well.
    Steam over the stock for 5 minutes. Remove the liver and vegetables, set
aside and keep warm. Add the honey and vinegar to the stock. Boil to reduce
until syrupy.
    Arrange the radiccio and watercress on four plates, then spoon on the liver
and vegetables. Pour on the sauce. Sprinkle with strips of ham and spring
onion tips, if liked. Serve at once.

WILD DUCK WITH CRACKED PEPPER AND APPLES

4 Granny Smith apples, peeled and
    cored but kept whole
juice of 1 lemon
1 tablespoon whole black
    peppercorns
600 ml/1 pint red wine
2 tablespoons Calvados brandy
2 shallots, finely chopped
4 wild duck breasts, wiped
salt
1 tablespoon olive oil
150 ml/¼ pint chicken or game stock
50 ml/2 fl oz double cream
sprigs of herbs to garnish, for
    example, chervil, flat-leaf parsley,
    fennel

*This is a recipe that is guaranteed to knock the taste buds into gear! If wild duck
is out of season, then domestic duck breasts work perfectly well. Feel free to
adjust the quantity of peppercorns to suit your palate: I like quite a powerful
flavour and the amount below was perfect for me.*

▶ Brush the apples with the lemon juice. Crush the peppercorns in a tea
towel with a mallet or rolling pin. Put the apples, peppercorns, wine,
Calvados, shallot and duck breasts in a shallow dish. Marinate for 2 hours,
turning the large pieces frequently.
    Remove the duck breasts and apples from the marinade and reserve the
liquid. Dry the duck on absorbent kitchen paper and sprinkle with a little salt.
Heat the oil in a heavy-based pan and fry the meat until golden brown on all
sides. Lay in the steamer with the apples. Bring the remaining marinade, stock
and cream to the boil. Steam the duck over the stock mixture for 10–12
minutes. Slice the apples. Arrange the duck and apples on a warmed serving
dish and keep hot. Reduce the peppered stock by boiling until syrupy. Taste
and adjust seasoning if necessary. Spoon the sauce over the duck and garnish
with sprigs of fresh garden herbs.

GROUSE WITH FIGS AND PORT SAUCE

8 large fresh figs
300 ml/½ pint ruby port
4 oven-ready grouse
1 tablespoon olive oil
4 shallots, finely chopped
1 celery stick, finely chopped
1 carrot, finely chopped
600 ml/1 pint chicken or game stock
1 teaspoon finely chopped thyme
100 g/4 oz tongue, cut into strips
salt and freshly ground black pepper
100 g/4 oz unsalted butter, cut into
    walnut-sized pieces
fresh fig leaves or bay leaves to
    serve
sprigs of thyme to garnish

This is my husband's favourite birthday recipe; luckily for him he was born in October when both grouse and figs are in season. Dried figs soaked in port will do admirably if you can't get fresh ones.

▶ Marinate the whole figs in the port for 24 hours. If you are short of time, simmer them gently in a pan for 10 minutes.

Cut the grouse in half. Heat the oil in a heavy-based frying pan and fry them on all sides until golden brown. Remove and set to one side. Fry the vegetables in the same pan until golden brown.

Drain the figs and place the port with the stock in a saucepan.

Lay a piece of foil in the steamer and arrange the grouse, vegetables and figs on top. Sprinkle with chopped thyme and tongue. Season well with salt and black pepper. Cover with a tight-fitting lid and steam over the port and stock for 35 minutes. *Check the liquid level frequently and add more boiling water if necessary.*

Arrange the food on fresh fig leaves and keep warm. Boil the stock to reduce until syrupy and whisk in the butter nut by nut until the sauce is creamy. Spoon the sauce over the grouse and serve garnished with thyme.

PHEASANT ON A DUXELLE OF WILD MUSHROOMS

4 breasts of pheasant
salt and freshly ground black pepper
2 tablespoons cherry jam
3 tablespoons red wine
2 tablespoons brandy
2 tablespoon Madeira or sherry
pinch of cinnamon
pinch of ground cloves
450 ml/¾ pint chicken or pheasant
    stock
1 kg/2 lb wild mushrooms, wiped
    and roughly chopped
1 clove garlic, crushed
Garnish
whole cherries
sliced mushrooms
flat-leaf parsley

Worry not, a duxelle using flat mushrooms is just as good, if you have searched the fields or streets for wild mushrooms to no avail. I love the combination of strong tasting pheasant with cherries and I am sure you will too. You may use cans of stoned black cherries if the jam is not available.

▶ Season the breasts with salt and freshly ground black pepper. Lay in a shallow dish with the cherry jam, wine, brandy, Madeira, cinnamon and cloves. Marinate for 2 hours.

Put the pheasant breasts to one side and bring the stock and all the marinade to the boil in a saucepan. Spread the mushrooms out in the steamer, sprinkle with garlic, salt and pepper. Arrange the marinated breasts on top. Cover with a tight fitting lid and steam over the stock for 20 minutes. *Check the liquid level frequently and add more boiling stock or water if necessary.*

Make a nest of mushrooms on four warmed plates; arrange the breasts on top. Keep warm. If the cherry stock is of the consistency of single cream then pour over the pheasant. If it is too thin then reduce by boiling until syrupy. Garnish with cherries, mushrooms and parsley.

STEAMED PHEASANT ON A NEST OF SAUERKRAUT

Sauerkraut, fermented white cabbage, is one of the most famous German foods and is usually sold in cans or jars. It was originally devised as a way of keeping white cabbage, which is packed with so many vitamins and minerals, throughout the winter months. The acidic flavour of sauerkraut combines beautifully with the gamey taste of the pheasant.

▶ Rinse and dry the pheasant. Remove the breast and legs from the birds. Chop the carcasses roughly and put in a pan with the carrot, celery and shallot. Pour on the red wine and stock or water. Bring to the boil and simmer gently for 2 hours. Pare the rind of the orange and cut into needleshreds.

Blanch for 20 seconds, keep to one side. Strain the stock into a saucepan, adding the juice of the orange, redcurrant jelly, port and mustard. Bring to the boil, remove any scum from the surface with a slotted spoon. Stir in the needleshreds. Season well with salt and freshly ground pepper.

Lay the sauerkraut over the base of the steamer. Heat the oil in a heavy-based pan and fry the pheasant over a high heat until golden brown on all sides. Season with salt and pepper. Arrange the pieces on top of the sauerkraut. Cover with a tightly fitting lid and steam over the stock for 20 minutes.

Remove the pheasant and sauerkraut from the steamer and keep warm. Reduce the sauce by boiling rapidly until rich and syrupy. Make a bed of sauerkraut on each plate. Arrange the pheasant pieces on top. Spoon over the sauce and decorate with fresh redcurrants and chopped parsley.

2 oven-ready pheasant
$\frac{1}{2}$ carrot, roughly chopped
1 celery stick, chopped
1 shallot, roughly chopped
300 ml/$\frac{1}{2}$ pint red wine
600 ml/1 pint chicken stock or water
rind and juice of 1 orange
100 g/4 oz redcurrant jelly
150 ml/$\frac{1}{4}$ pint ruby port
1 teaspoon French mustard
salt and freshly ground black pepper
225 g/8 oz sauerkraut
1 tablespoon olive oil
Garnish
fresh redcurrants
chopped parsley

FOOD FACTS

▶ There are a few rules to remember if you are trying to follow a healthy diet plan: avoid eating too much fat, sugar and salt. Include plenty of fresh foods and fibre-rich items in your meals. This is just an outline of points that are worth considering.

Poultry and game can contribute to this plan by providing ample protein without too much fat. In the case of duck, the fat can be drained off during cooking and the skin can be removed from poultry before serving.

Both poultry and game are available as fresh, naturally produced foods that are free from additives. In the case of chicken you will have to buy carefully but game is additive-free and low in fat.

To maintain the low-fat status of these foods the cooking method is important and steaming is a good option.

Whenever you are steaming chicken it is important to check that the bird is cooked through. Simply pierce the flesh at the thickest part – usually on the thigh joint – and look out for any traces of blood in the juices. If there are any signs of blood the bird is not ready and further cooking is required.

SLICED PIGEON BREASTS WITH LIME

4 oven-ready wood pigeons, breasts
  removed
1 small carrot, roughly chopped
1 celery stick, roughly chopped
1 shallot, roughly chopped
sprigs of thyme
300 ml/½ pint red wine
2 limes
4 spring onions, trimmed and finely
  sliced
2 celery sticks, cut into matchsticks
100 g/4 oz mangetout, topped and
  tailed
4 tablespoons redcurrant jelly
salt and freshly ground black pepper
Garnish
needleshreds of lime
sprigs of flat-leaf parsley or coriander

Game often cries out for acidic sauces. Lime and pigeon is a great success.

▶ The breasts are removed by sliding a sharp knife either side of the breastbone. Roughly chop the carcasses and fry in a saucepan with the carrot, celery and shallot until golden brown. Add the thyme, red wine and enough water to just cover the birds. Bring to the boil, cover and simmer for 2 hours: this will be your stock.

Meanwhile, pare the rind of half a lime and cut into needleshreds, then blanch in boiling water for 20 seconds. Keep to one side. Remove the pith from the limes with a sharp knife. Cut the flesh into segments reserving the juice. Strain the stock into the saucepan. Bring to the boil and remove any scum from the surface. Add the segments of one lime to the stock. Lay a sheet of greaseproof paper over the base of the steamer. Arrange the spring onion, celery, mangetout and remaining lime segments on top. Using a knife, spread the breasts with redcurrant jelly. Season well. Cover with a tight fitting lid and steam over the stock for 15 minutes. *Check the liquid level frequently and add boiling stock if necessary.*

Arrange the meat and vegetables on four warmed plates, and keep hot. Reduce the stock by boiling rapidly until syrupy. Pour over the breasts, and garnish with needleshreds of lime and parsley or coriander sprigs.

GUINEA FOWL WITH FRESH MARKET VEGETABLES

2 oven-ready guinea fowl, cut in half
  lengthways
salt and freshly ground black pepper
juice of 1 lemon
2 tablespoons olive oil
1 tablespoon chopped fresh sage
1 tablespoon chopped chives
2 cloves garlic, crushed
600 ml/1 pint chicken stock
1 yellow pepper, deseeded and cut
  into thick matchsticks
50 g/2 oz mangetout, topped and
  tailed
50 g/2 oz green beans, topped and
  tailed, cut into three pieces
2 carrots, cut into thick matchsticks
8 radishes
50 g/2 oz fromage frais
chopped chives to garnish

The colour and crispness of the vegetables and the flavour of the succulent guinea fowl, slightly reminiscent of pheasant, combine beautifully with an outstanding sauce.

▶ Rinse and dry the guinea fowl. Season the fowl with salt and black pepper and lemon juice. Heat the oil in a heavy-based pan. Fry the guinea fowl until golden brown on both sides. Lay a piece of wet greaseproof paper in the steamer. Arrange the guinea fowl on the top. Sprinkle with the sage, chives and garlic.

Pour the stock into the same frying pan. Bring to the boil, scraping the sediment from the base of the pan. Pour into a saucepan. Cover the food with a tight fitting lid and steam over the stock for 20 minutes. *Check the liquid level frequently and add more boiling stock or water if necessary.* Add the vegetables to the guinea fowl and cook for 5 minutes.

Keep the fowl and vegetables warm to one side, whilst finishing the sauce. Boil the stock to reduce until syrupy. Stir in the fromage frais. Taste and adjust seasoning if necessary. Serve the guinea fowl on a bed of vegetables, garnished with chopped chives. Serve the sauce separately.

LIGHT MEAT DISHES

Meat seems to have got a poor press recently. However, it remains a major supplier of nutrients including protein, some of the B vitamins, and iron. The offal is usually the healthiest part of the animal to eat, being relatively low in fat and usually containing a high proportion of vitamins and minerals. The most tender cuts of meat are the parts of the animal that move least, and therefore the toughest are the legs, neck and shoulder. Steaming meat has two advantages over other forms of cooking: firstly you retain all the valuable nutrients and goodness; and secondly, never again will you have to put up with stringy meat in casseroles that have accidentally boiled. This is all because steaming is such a steady and gentle cooking method. I have set out to provide innovative, light recipes in which vegetables and sauces play an important accompanying role.

Lamb en Papillote (page 38)

BROWN BONE STOCK

marrow bones, for example, beef,
     veal, duck
pieces of raw meat (except lamb)
1 onion
1 turnip
1 carrot
1 celery stick
mushroom trimmings
oil or dripping
6 parsley stalks
2 bay leaves
pinch of thyme
10 black peppercorns
300–600 ml/½–1 pint red or white
     wine

*Use any raw meat bones except for raw lamb bones as they have a strong
flavour which could well spoil your intended dish. Cooked lamb bones
however work perfectly well. Mix the bones for mixed stock, or keep separate
for single flavour stocks.*

▶ Ask the butcher to break up the bones. Brown them well in the oven. Peel
the vegetables, reserving the parings, and finely chop. Heat the oil in a large
stock pot and fry the vegetables until brown. Add the bones and all the
remaining ingredients including the peelings. Pour on enough water to cover
the bones. Bring to the boil and simmer very gently for 4 hours, skimming off
any scum from the surface occasionally. *Check liquid level frequently and add
more boiling water if necessary.* Strain the stock through cloth or a fine sieve,
allowing it to drip. If a stronger stock is required, bring the strained stock back
to the boil and boil rapidly to reduce.

WHITE BONE STOCK
▶ Follow the recipe for brown bone stock, but do not brown the bones and
vegetables prior to using. White stocks are used for cream sauces and white
stews.

CHICKEN STOCK
▶ Follow the recipe for brown and white bone stock and use the giblets
(except for the liver) as well as the carcass.

FILLET OF BEEF WITH
HORSERADISH AND BASIL

450 g/1 lb extra-lean minced beef
1 egg white
2 teaspoons freshly grated
     horseradish or horseradish sauce
1 tablespoon chopped fresh basil
2 shallots, very finely chopped
2 teaspoons cornflour
salt and freshly ground black pepper
sprigs of basil to garnish
Tomato Sauce
1 (400-g/14-oz) can chopped
     tomatoes
2 cloves garlic, peeled and crushed
1 tablespoon chopped fresh basil
150 ml/¼ pint beef stock

*A selection of best-cut meat balls. The secret of making them light and fluffy lies
in the egg white and cornflour. If you find the best cut such as fillet of beef and
loin of lamb a little steep on the purse then use any other lean cut. Make sure
that you remove all visible fat.*

▶ Mix the beef in a liquidiser or food processor for a few seconds. Slowly add
the egg white, horseradish and basil. Mix for a few seconds until they are fully
incorporated into the meat. Add the shallot and cornflour. Season well with
salt and black pepper.
   Dust your hands with cornflour and form the mixture into 3.5-cm/1½-in
balls – about the size of a golf ball. Place all the ingredients for the tomato
sauce in a saucepan and bring to the boil. Put the meatballs in the steamer.
Cover with a tight fitting lid and steam over the sauce for 10 minutes. Divide
meatballs between four warmed serving plates, keep warm. Place the tomato
sauce in a liquidiser or food processor and blend until smooth.
   Taste and adjust seasoning if necessary. Pour over the meatballs and
garnish with sprigs of basil.

PEPPERED TENDERLOIN WITH MUSTARD AND SPINACH

A tender, succulent piece of beef with a rich pepper and mustard sauce, served on a bed of spinach. A word of warning; you should ventilate your kitchen when you make this recipe, as the odour of frying peppercorns could sting your eyes or make you sneeze. Do not be put off however, because I can assure you that it is well worth it in the end. Keep your eye on the cooking time as it would be a great pity to overcook the beef.

50 g/2 oz black peppercorns
1.75 kg/4 lb beef tenderloin, trimmed
3 teaspoons Dijon mustard
2 tablespoons oil
300 ml/$\frac{1}{2}$ pint beef stock
300 ml/$\frac{1}{2}$ pint red wine
2 tablespoons brandy
225 g/8 oz spinach, washed and
large stalks discarded
100 g/4 oz unsalted butter, cut into
walnut-sized pieces

▶ Place the peppercorns in a plastic bag or tea towel. Crush with a mallet or rolling pin.

Spread the tenderloin with 2 teaspoons of the mustard and cover all sides with the crushed peppercorns. Heat the oil until very hot in a heavy-based pan. Fry the peppered beef to seal all of the edges. Remove from the pan and set aside. Pour the beef stock, red wine and brandy into the frying pan. Bring to the boil scraping the sediment from the base of the pan. Pour into a saucepan and stir in the remaining mustard. Bring to the boil.

Cut a piece of foil large enough to seal the meat completely. Arrange the spinach on the foil and place the meat on top. Fold up the edges and seal completely. Put the food in the steamer. Cover with a tight fitting lid and steam over the stock mixture for 30 minutes.

Remove the meat parcel and leave to one side whilst finishing the sauce. Reduce the stock by boiling rapidly until syrupy. Lower the heat and whisk the butter in nut by nut until the sauce is creamy.

Slice the beef and arrange with the spinach on four individual plates. Spoon over the sauce and serve immediately.

FOOD FACTS

▶ The tendency these days is towards eating less meat, selecting the leaner cuts and combining them with light sauces and crisp vegetables.

Steaming can be an excellent cooking method for meat, providing tender results and flavoursome sauces. Follow the advice on page 123 when selecting and buying meat. You will find that recipes in this chapter offer plenty of ideas for dishes that are delicious yet quite light, with the emphasis on serving cooking juices rather than rich sauces.

Offal is a food that is rich in nutrients and low in fat. More information on the preparation of offal is included on page 68. Here you will find suggestions for creating unusual, delicious dishes based on sweetbreads, brains, liver and kidneys.

So if you are aiming at improving your diet and feel concerned about the amount of meat you eat,

then remember to balance it with other ingredients – include fresh fish and seafood, poultry, offal, rice and grains as alternative sources of protein. Trim fat from the meat before cooking and skim fat from sauces before they are served. If your diet is full of variety the chances are that you are adopting a fairly healthy approach.

LAMB EN PAPILLOTE

150 ml/¼ pint lamb stock
2 tablespoons red wine
8 lamb cutlets, fat removed
salt and freshly ground black pepper
1 tablespoon olive oil
1 onion, finely chopped
175 g/6 oz fresh runner beans,
    topped, tailed and cut into bite-
    sized pieces
175 g/6 oz podded broad beans
100 g/4 oz podded fresh or frozen
    peas
4 teaspoons mint sauce
2 teaspoons redcurrant jelly
small sprigs of rosemary
2 cloves of garlic, finely chopped

A healthy pouch of sweet lamb with fresh garden vegetables. I like this recipe because all of the goodness is cooked into the food and not allowed to escape.

▶ Boil the stock and red wine until syrupy. Season the cutlets of lamb with salt and black pepper. Heat the oil in a heavy-based pan, and fry the cutlets until golden brown on all sides. Remove them from the pan and set aside. Fry the onion in the same pan until cooked but not brown. Pour in the stock and bring to the boil, scraping any sediment from the base of the pan. Keep to one side. Steam the vegetables for 3 minutes then plunge them in cold water.

Cut four 35-cm/14-in-square pieces of foil. Arrange two lamb cutlets and a quarter of the vegetables on each piece of foil. Divide the mint sauce, redcurrant jelly, the sprigs of rosemary and garlic between each portion. Fold up the sides but leave open. Spoon on the stock and onions and season well with salt and freshly ground black pepper. Seal the parcels completely. Place in the steamer. Cover with a tight fitting lid and steam over boiling water for 15 minutes. Serve immediately.

Allow your guests to open the parcels at the table.

LEG OF LAMB WITH HERBS

1 teaspoon oil
1 small onion, chopped
2 leeks, trimmed, washed and finely
    sliced
100 g/4 oz salsify, peeled and
    chopped
2 large cloves garlic, crushed
1 (1-kg/2-lb) lean leg of lamb, boned
150 ml/¼ pint lamb or beef stock
1½ tablespoons redcurrant jelly
sprigs of rosemary
sprigs of mint
salt and freshly ground black pepper
sprigs of rosemary or mint to
    garnish

Steamed meat cooks gently and quickly but you must take care not to over or underdo it. The lamb should be a little pink when removed from the steamer and must be eaten at once. This recipe is a healthier version of the traditional Sunday lunch, and I think the texture and flavour here are better than those of any roasted meat.

▶ Heat the oil in a heavy-based pan, fry the onion, leek, salsify and garlic for 3 minutes. Cut a piece of foil large enough to seal the meat and vegetables completely. Spoon the vegetables into the centre of the foil. Fry the meat over a high heat to brown on all sides. Place on top of the vegetables.

Pour the stock into the frying pan and bring to the boil scraping all sediment from the base of the pan. Fold the edges of foil up around the meat. Pour in the stock. Add the redcurrant jelly, rosemary and mint, season with salt and freshly ground black pepper, seal completely. Place in a steamer, cover with a tight fitting lid and steam over boiling water for 1 hour. *Check the liquid every 15 minutes and add more boiling water if necessary.*

Remove the lamb and allow it to sit for 10 minutes, meanwhile pour the vegetables and stock into a saucepan and boil to reduce until syrupy. Taste and adjust the seasoning if necessary.

Slice the lamb into 1-cm/½-in slices; arrange on a warmed serving dish and pour the sauce over the lamb. Garnish with sprigs of rosemary or mint.

From the top: Marinated Pork Fillets with Fresh Garden Herbs (page 40); Leg of Lamb with Herbs

MINCED LAMB WITH THYME FLOWERS

450 g/1 lb lean lamb, minced
1 egg white
1 tablespoon redcurrant jelly
½ teaspoon fresh thyme flowers and
  leaves from sprigs of thyme
2 cloves garlic, crushed
4 spring onions, trimmed and finely
  chopped
1 teaspoon cornflour
salt and freshly ground black pepper
300 ml/½ pint lamb or beef stock
sprigs of thyme
8 baby carrots
8 baby turnips, peeled
50 g/2 oz mangetout, topped and
  tailed
8 radishes, tailed
100 g/4 oz unsalted butter, cut into
  walnut-sized pieces
sprigs of flowering thyme or flat-leaf
  parsley to garnish

The best thyme comes from scrublands, not far from the sea. They spring up after the last frosts of the winter and cover the hills with blue or pink flowers. The flowers last only for about two weeks in May. Use plain fresh thyme when the flowers are not available.

▶ Blend the lamb in the liquidiser or food processor for a few seconds. Slowly add the egg white, redcurrant jelly and thyme flowers and leaves. Process for a few more seconds until they are fully incorporated into the meat. Mix in the garlic, spring onion and cornflour; season well with salt and freshly ground black pepper. Dust your hands with cornflour and form the mixture into 3.5-cm/1½-in balls. Bring the stock to the boil in a saucepan. Place the meatballs, thyme sprigs and vegetables in the steamer. Cover with a tight fitting lid and steam over the stock for 10 minutes.

Arrange the food on four warmed plates and keep warm. Boil the stock to reduce until syrupy. Whisk in the butter, nut by nut until the sauce is creamy and smooth. Pour over the meatballs and vegetables. Garnish with flowering thyme or flat-leaf parsley.

MARINATED PORK FILLETS WITH FRESH GARDEN HERBS

8 (150-g/5-oz) pork fillets
salt and freshly ground black pepper
300 ml/½ pint red wine
juice of 1 lemon
3 tablespoons chopped fresh mixed
  herbs, for example, sage, oregano,
  marjoram, thyme, parsley
1 kg/2 lb leeks, trimmed washed and
  finely sliced
100 g/4 oz Gruyère cheese, grated
1 tablespoon oil
300 ml/½ pint pork or chicken stock
1 tablespoon apple sauce
Garnish
2 tablespoons chopped fresh herbs,
  for example, parsley, sage,
  oregano, marjoram, thyme
  (optional)
red and green-skinned apple slices
  (optional)

Beautiful rolls of pork smothered with chopped fresh herbs, but what I love more about this dish is the mouthwatering layers of oozing cheese in the centre.

▶ Beat each pork fillet flat between two sheets of wet greaseproof paper with a mallet or rolling pin. Season both sides well.

Lay the fillets in a dish with the red wine, lemon juice and 1 tablespoon of the herbs. Marinate for up to 2 hours. Lay a piece of wet greaseproof paper in the steamer. Spread the sliced leeks on top.

Remove the fillets from the marinade. Sprinkle the cheese evenly over each fillet, then roll up. Heat the oil in a heavy-based pan and fry the pork rolls to brown on all sides. Lay side by side on top of the leeks and sprinkle with the remaining herbs. Bring the stock, remainder of the marinade, and the apple sauce to the boil in the pan in which the pork rolls were browned, scraping the sediment from the base of the pan. Pour into a saucepan, cover the food with a tight fitting lid and steam over the stock mixture for 20 minutes. Arrange the pork rolls and leeks on four warmed plates, keep hot. Boil the sauce to reduce until syrupy. Taste and adjust seasoning if necessary.

Pour over the meat rolls, sprinkle with mixed herbs and garnish with apple slices, if liked and serve at once.

VEAL PURSES

A delicate mixture of veal with lemon and aromatic vegetables in a light pancake pouch. Vegetable combinations can be selected for this recipe according to the season. Pancakes freeze well, if separated with pieces of greaseproof paper, and so can be made in advance.

▶ Place the veal in a shallow dish, mix the cornflour with the lemon juice to a smooth cream. Add the white wine and pour over the veal. Leave to marinate for 1–2 hours.

Meanwhile, make the pancakes. Place all the pancake ingredients in a liquidiser, blend for 10 seconds until the mixture looks smooth and creamy. Refrigerate for 30 minutes. Prepare the pancake pan by heating well and wiping out with oil. Pour in about 1 tablespoon of batter and swirl about the pan until evenly spread across the bottom. Place over high heat for 30 seconds–1 minute. Turn the pancake over by using a palette knife. Cook until brown. Make all the pancakes, turning them out onto a plate.

Place 150 ml/¼ pint of the veal stock and all the marinade in a pan, having put the veal strips to one side. Bring to the boil and reduce until thick and syrupy, stirring constantly. Blanch the vegetables for 10 seconds in boiling water. Mix the veal strips, the sauce and three-quarters of the vegetables together. Season well with salt and freshly ground black pepper.

Wrap up equal amounts of the mixture in twelve pancakes. Arrange side by side in the steamer. Bring the remaining stock to the boil. Cover the food with a tight fitting lid and steam over the stock for 10 minutes.

Arrange three purses on each plate and keep warm. Reduce the stock by boiling rapidly until syrupy. Serve with the parcels separately. Garnish the purses with the remaining vegetables. Eat at once.

4 (150-g/5-oz) veal escalopes, cut
  into strips, fat discarded
2 teaspoons cornflour
juice of 1 lemon
6 tablespoons white wine
Pancake Ingredients
100 g/4 oz plain flour, sifted
pinch of salt
1 egg, beaten
150 ml/¼ pint milk
150 ml/¼ pint water
1 tablespoon oil
450 ml/¾ pint veal stock
50 g/2 oz mangetout
75 g/3 oz salsify, peeled and cut into
  strips
4 spring onions, trimmed and finely
  chopped
1 carrot, cut into strips
salt and freshly ground black pepper

FOOD FACTS

▶ Pancakes do freeze well, so if you have the time, make a large batch. Keep the pancakes separate by layering cling film or special freezer separating leaves between each one. Freeze the pancakes packed flat, then when you want to remove any simply slide a palette knife between each one.

CALF'S SWEETBREADS WITH SPINACH AND COURGETTES

575 g/1¼ lb calf's sweetbreads
450 g/1 lb courgettes, cut into
  matchsticks
salt and freshly ground black pepper
1 tablespoon olive oil
2 shallots, finely chopped
75 g/3 oz rindless smoked bacon,
  diced
300 ml/½ pint veal or beef stock
½ tablespoon red wine vinegar
450 g/1 lb spinach, washed, and
  large stalks discarded
sprigs of flat-leaf parsley to garnish
  (optional)

Calf's sweetbreads are sold in pairs and have a soft, creamy texture with a delicate flavour.

As they may be in short supply, you can easily use the smaller lamb's sweetbreads as an alternative.

▶ Cover and soak the calf's sweetbreads for several hours, changing the water frequently. Place the courgette matchsticks in a colander, sprinkle with salt and leave for 30 minutes. Heat the oil in a pan, and fry the shallot and bacon until golden brown. Blanch the sweetbreads in boiling water for 5–10 minutes. Refresh in cold water and remove the skin with small knife. Rinse the courgette matchsticks under cold water to remove all of the salt.

Bring the veal stock and vinegar to the boil in a saucepan. Arrange the spinach, courgette, shallot, bacon and sweetbreads in the steamer on top. Season well. Cover with a tight fitting lid and steam over the stock for 20–25 minutes. Remove and slice the sweetbreads, then arrange the food on four individual plates and keep warm. Boil the stock to reduce until syrupy. Pour over the sweetbreads, and garnish with parsley sprigs if liked.

MINCED VEAL WITH GREEN PEPPERCORNS

1 tablespoon olive oil
1 small onion, finely chopped
¼ red pepper, deseeded and diced
2 cloves garlic, crushed
275 g/10 oz lean pie-veal, minced,
  fat removed
75 g/3 oz podded broad beans, finely
  chopped
50 g/2 oz fresh or frozen sweetcorn
1 tablespoon chopped parsley
1 generous teaspoon well rinsed
  green peppercorns
salt and freshly ground black pepper
8 large Chinese lettuce leaves
Sauce
300 ml/½ pint boiling veal or chicken
  stock
2 tablespoons white wine vinegar
  with green peppercorns
1 teaspoon well rinsed green
  peppercorns
1 teaspoon honey

This veal recipe has a colourful mixture of fresh vegetables which can be wrapped tightly in a diverse selection of leaves, for example Savoy cabbage or radiccio leaves. Strips of red pepper and chopped parsley can be used for garnish, if liked.

Green peppercorns come in cans or jars, and you must make sure that you rinse them thoroughly under cold running water to remove the salt. If you do not have green peppercorn vinegar, then soak 1 teaspoon of well rinsed peppercorns in 150 ml/¼ pint white wine vinegar and leave to stand overnight if possible.

▶ Heat the oil in a pan. Gently fry the onion, diced red pepper and garlic until cooked but not brown. Stir in the veal, broad beans, sweetcorn, parsley and peppercorns. Season well with salt and freshly ground black pepper. Fry for 4 minutes, stirring well. Steam the Chinese leaves over the boiling stock for 20 seconds or until just limp.

Divide the mixture between the eight leaves and wrap up tightly. Lay side by side in the steamer. Season the outside of the leaves with salt and pepper. Cover with a tight fitting lid and steam over the stock for 10 minutes. Arrange two lettuce parcels on each plate. Keep warm.

Reduce the veal or chicken stock until rich and syrupy. Stir in the vinegar, green peppercorns and honey. Taste and adjust seasoning if necessary. Pour over the parcels and serve.

CALF'S BRAINS WITH BLACK BUTTER

4 calf's brains (or lamb's brains)
juice of 1 lemon
300 ml/$\frac{1}{2}$ pint court bouillon (page 14)
salt and freshly ground black pepper
75 g/3 oz unsalted butter
1 tablespoon capers
1 shallot, finely chopped
$\frac{1}{2}$ tablespoon caper or white wine vinegar
1 tablespoon chopped parsley to garnish

Calf's brains are an expensive delicacy. They have an exquisite delicate flavour and creamy texture, but are quite difficult to get hold of, so you could use the more readily available lamb's brains instead.

Brains, like sweetbreads must be soaked in cold water for a few hours. The water needs to be changed regularly to remove all blood.

Black butter is the most popular sauce to serve with brains.

▶ Soak the brains in water with the lemon juice for 2–3 hours. Drain them. Bring the court bouillon to the boil in a saucepan. Arrange the brains in the steamer. Cover with a tight fitting lid, and steam over the bouillon for 15 minutes. Cut the brains into slices, removing any membranes. Lay on a heated serving dish, season with salt and pepper, and keep them warm.

Heat the butter in a pan until brown but not burnt. Stir in the capers, shallot and vinegar. Bring to the boil and pour over the brains. Sprinkle with parsley and serve immediately.

CALF'S LIVER SPIKED WITH MUSTARD AND SAGE

350 g/12 oz calf's liver, trimmed
175–225 g/6–8 oz fresh white or brown breadcrumbs
1 egg white
4 teaspoons Dijon mustard
1 teaspoon chopped fresh sage
2 shallots, very finely chopped
5 teaspoons cornflour
salt and freshly ground black pepper
15 g/$\frac{1}{2}$ oz butter
2 cloves garlic, crushed
450 g/1 lb mushrooms, wiped and finely chopped
300 ml/$\frac{1}{2}$ pint veal or beef stock
100 g/4 oz unsalted butter cut into walnut-sized pieces
sprigs of sage to garnish

Lamb's liver will do perfectly well for this recipe as well as being slightly cheaper; however the flavour is much more delicate with calf's liver.

▶ Mix the liver with enough breadcrumbs in the liquidiser or food processor to form a smooth paste. Add the egg white, 2 teaspoons of the mustard and $\frac{1}{2}$ teaspoon of the sage. Mix them for a few seconds until they are thoroughly incorporated into the meat. Mix in the shallot and the cornflour. Season well with salt and freshly ground black pepper.

Dust your hands with cornflour and form the mixture into 3.5-cm/1$\frac{1}{2}$-in balls – about the size of a golf ball. Heat the butter in a pan, fry the garlic and chopped mushrooms for 2 minutes.

Bring the stock to the boil in a saucepan. Lay a piece of wet greaseproof paper in the steamer. Spread the chopped mushrooms on top. Arrange the liver balls on the mushrooms, cover with a tight fitting lid and steam over the stock for 6 minutes.

Arrange the meatballs on four warmed serving plates and keep warm.

Stir the mushrooms and any meat juices into the stock. Add the remaining mustard and sage. Boil rapidly to reduce until syrupy. Whisk in the butter, nut by nut until the sauce is creamy.

Pour over meatballs, garnish with sprigs of sage and serve at once.

LAMB'S LIVER WITH BABY ONIONS AND CHIVE SAUCE

A delicious and economical dish of tender steamed lamb's liver with whole baby onions on a light chive sauce. The texture of delicately steamed liver will completely eliminate those dreadful memories of 'school liver'.

▶ Season the strips of liver with salt and pepper. Lay in a dish with the lemon juice, sherry, honey, onions and 1 tablespoon of the chives. Marinate for up to 2 hours. Cut a piece of foil or greaseproof paper large enough to seal all of the ingredients in a large parcel.

Spoon the food on to the foil. Fold up the edges, pour in all of the marinade and seal completely. Place in the steamer. Bring the stock and remaining chives to the boil in a saucepan. Cover the steamer with a tight fitting lid and steam over the stock for 10 minutes. Remove the foil and pour the juices from the meat into the stock. Keep the food warm to one side whilst finishing the sauce.

Boil the stock until syrupy, then reduce the heat. Whisk in the butter, nut by nut, until the sauce is creamy. Turn off the heat. Arrange the liver and onions on four warmed plates. Pour over the sauce and garnish with bacon dice and chopped chives. Serve at once.

450 g/1 lb lamb's liver, trimmed and
    cut into strips
salt and freshly ground black pepper
juice of $\frac{1}{2}$ lemon
2 tablespoons sherry
$\frac{1}{2}$ teaspoon honey
16 button onions
3 tablespoons chopped chives
150 ml/$\frac{1}{4}$ pint beef stock
50 g/2 oz butter, cut into walnut-
    sized pieces
Garnish
50 g/2 oz cooked rindless smoked
    bacon, cut into dice
1 tablespoon chopped chives

KIDNEYS WITH HOT PEPPER SAUCE AND BACON COULIS

You have the choice between veal, lamb, pig and ox when you buy kidneys, and any of these will do. However, I think that the tender and delicately flavoured veal kidneys are probably the best, but they are of course the most expensive.

▶ Cut the kidneys into bite-sized pieces. Lay in a dish with the orange and lemon juice, brandy, salt and pepper. Marinate for 2 hours.

Roughly chop one and a half peppers and cut the remaining half pepper into fine strips for the garnish. Place the roughly chopped red pepper pieces, chilli, stock, tomato purée and three-quarters of the bacon strips into a saucepan. Stir in all of the marinade. Bring to the boil. Arrange the kidneys on a piece of wet greaseproof paper in the steamer. Cover with a tight fitting lid and steam over the pepper mixture for 7 minutes. Grill the remaining bacon strips for garnish.

Arrange the kidneys on four warmed plates and keep warm. Blend the pepper mixture in a liquidiser or food processor until smooth. Taste and adjust seasoning if necessary.

Spoon the sauce over the kidneys, decorate with thin strips of red pepper and cooked bacon. Serve at once.

450 g/1 lb kidneys, trimmed of fat
    and core
juice of 1 orange
juice of 1 lemon
1 tablespoon brandy
salt and freshly ground black pepper
2 red peppers, deseeded
2 green or red chillies, deseeded
    and finely chopped
150 ml/$\frac{1}{4}$ pint veal stock
1 tablespoon tomato purée
100 g/4 oz rindless smoked bacon,
    cut into strips
Garnish
thin strips of red pepper
thin strips of cooked bacon

VERSATILE VEGETABLES

Vegetable eating is on the increase due to the growing interest in nutrition and recommendations to reduce fat intake and increase fibre in the diet. Vegetables are the principal source of cellulose and fibre and contain vitamins and minerals not commonly available in other foods. They also play a vital part in food presentation: a colourful vegetable selection will add immeasurably to the look of a dish. To gain maximum nutritional benefits, vegetables should not be stored for too long. Avoid soaking in water as vitamin C is water soluble and make sure you cut or peel vegetables just before using; it is escaping vitamin C that turns apples and potatoes brown. Some cooking methods can ruin nutritional benefits: boiling a vegetable for 8–10 minutes causes 65–80% loss of vitamin C and phosphorus. However, steaming retains 80% of the vitamin C content, as well as colour, flavour and shape. The following recipes form a complete meal if served with some cheese and/or crusty wholemeal bread, otherwise they can simply be served to accompany a main course.

Nest of Baby Vegetables (opposite)

RAINBOW OF SEASONAL VEGETABLES

As vegetables play a large part in our diet today, choose a selection of interesting colours and textures to whet your appetite. This recipe makes the perfect accompaniment to all meat, or serve just on its own sprinkled with grated cheese and grilled until golden brown, and served with crusty fresh bread.

▶ Mix the butter with the herbs and season well. Place the courgette, leek, carrot, beans and celery in a steamer, season well with salt and black pepper.

Cover and steam over boiling water for 3–5 minutes. Add the watercress and steam for 1 minute. Turn on to a warmed serving dish and dot with herb butter.

50 g/2 oz butter
1 tablespoon chopped fresh herbs, for example, mint, parsley
salt and freshly ground black pepper
4 courgettes, cut in half lengthways
2 leeks, trimmed, washed, and thickly sliced
2 large carrots, cut into thick matchsticks
100 g/4 oz French beans, topped and tailed
4 celery sticks, cut into thick matchsticks
small bunch of watercress, washed

NEST OF BABY VEGETABLES

A pouch of colourful, crisp, nutritious vegetables. The vegetables are left whole so that none of the vitamins and minerals can escape. Let your guests open the envelopes at the table. This is an ideal accompaniment for any meat, fish, poultry or game.

▶ Fold eight sheets of greaseproof paper in half, and cut a semi-circle of 15 cm/6 in radius through each so that when opened out you have eight 30 cm/12 in rounds of paper.

Place the circles together in pairs so that you have four double-thick circles.

Divide all of the ingredients between the four circles, arranging the food on one half of each circle only, and season well with salt and freshly ground black pepper. Fold the free half over to make a parcel rather like an apple turnover. Fold the edges of the layers of paper over twice together, twisting and pressing hard to make an air-tight seal.

Lay the parcels inside the steamer. Cover with a tight fitting lid and steam over boiling water for 8–10 minutes.

Serve at once.

12 baby carrots, washed
12 baby turnips, washed
50 g/2 oz mangetout, topped and tailed
100 g/4 oz French beans, topped and tailed
8 button onions
8 radishes, washed
50 g/2 oz butter
4 tablespoons white wine
4 strips lemon zest
4 teaspoons chopped fresh herbs, for example, chervil, chives, mint
salt and freshly ground black pepper

A TRIO OF COULIS

Carrot Coulis
225 g/8 oz carrots, finely sliced
150 ml/¼ pint orange juice
50 g/2 oz fromage frais or quark
salt and freshly ground black pepper
pinch of ground coriander
1 teaspoon lemon juice

Brussels Sprout Coulis
225 g/8 oz Brussels sprouts, trimmed
    and sliced
150 ml/¼ pint vegetable or chicken
    stock
50 g/2 oz fromage frais or quark
1 teaspoon lemon juice
½ teaspoon chopped mint
salt and freshly ground black pepper

Parsnip Coulis
225 g/8 oz parsnips, peeled and
    finely sliced
150 ml/¼ pint vegetable or chicken
    stock
50 g/2 oz fromage frais or quark
1 teaspoon lemon juice
salt and freshly ground black pepper
pinch of freshly grated nutmeg

This stunning vegetable combination is an effective accompaniment to lightly steamed fish. It is easy to digest and a joy to eat.

I have chosen the vegetables below for their perfect contrast of colours and flavours. You may however use any vegetables, but bear in mind the overall look of the dish; in other words if you choose three green vegetables, it will be delicious but the overall effect will be lost. To save time, cook the vegetables separately but at the same time.

▶ Steam the carrots over the orange juice for 10 minutes. Blend with the juice in a liquidiser, stir in the fromage frais or quark and season with salt, pepper, coriander and lemon juice. Taste and adjust seasoning if necessary. Cover and keep warm to one side.

Steam the Brussels sprouts over the stock for 10 minutes. Blend with the stock in the liquidiser, and stir in the fromage frais or quark, lemon juice and mint. Season with salt and black pepper. Taste and adjust seasoning if necessary. Cover and keep warm to one side.

Steam the parsnip over the stock for 10 minutes. Blend with the stock in the liquidiser, and stir in the fromage frais or quark and lemon juice. Season well with salt, pepper and nutmeg. Cover and keep warm.

To serve, spoon the Brussels sprout and parsnip coulis next to each other on each warmed plate. Garnish with the carrot coulis to your own design. Top with steamed fish or meat.

Serve at once.

FOOD FACTS

▶ Fresh vegetables need little introduction for the contribution they have to make towards healthy eating.

The recipes in this chapter prove that vegetables can be used to create a range of exciting, colourful dishes that taste quite superb. Here you will discover that healthy eating is by no means boring.

As well as offering fibre, vegetables supply vitamins – notably A and C – and minerals. Certain green vegetables also provide a valuable source of iron,

calcium and vitamin B_1. Away from the hard facts, cooked and presented well, vegetables contribute texture and colour that is essential in creating successful meals.

Steaming is an ideal method of cooking vegetables since it ensures the maximum retention of water-soluble nutrients that would otherwise be lost into the cooking liquid. In addition to this welcome retention of nutrients, steaming results in vegetables that have an excellent colour and shape.

It is a method that can be closely controlled to produce crisp, perfectly cooked food. Given that the pieces of food are of an equal size, then they will all be evenly cooked.

Prepare the vegetables according to their type but it is preferable not to peel potatoes. Arrange them in the steaming compartment and cook over boiling water or any suitable main dish. Carefully peel potatoes after cooking, if preferred. Serve the vegetables with butter and chopped fresh herbs, or

use herb butter; alternatively offer a Hollandaise sauce as an accompaniment. The cooking time will depend on the size of the vegetables and the result required. For potatoes allow about 25 minutes, similarly for other root vegetables that should be quite tender when served. For crisp results allow brief cooking, bearing in mind the time you would normally allow for boiling and adding a little extra.

SPINACH LOAF ON YELLOW PEPPERS

This dish is exceptionally pretty with its wonderful contrast of flavours and colours. Use as a first course, or for a light lunch serve with salad and crusty brown bread.

It can be made in advance and served hot or cold.

▶ Melt the butter in a pan and fry the garlic and leek until soft but not brown. Season with salt and pepper. Steam the spinach leaves until just limp, about 10 seconds. Remove 15 of the best leaves and dry on absorbent kitchen paper. Squeeze all water from remaining spinach between two plates, and chop the spinach finely.

Butter a 450-g/1-lb loaf tin and line with the spinach leaves. Stir the chopped spinach into the leeks. Remove from heat and add the breadcrumbs, eggs, egg yolk and nutmeg; season well with salt and pepper.

Heat the milk to just before boiling and stir it into the vegetable mixture. Spoon into the prepared loaf tin. Cover with greased foil or greaseproof paper and tie down. Cover with a tight fitting lid and steam very gently over water that is barely boiling for 50–60 minutes. If the mixture gets too hot the eggs will scramble causing the loaf to curdle.

Meanwhile make the sauce. Put the yellow pepper, lemon juice, shallot and stock in a pan, bring to the boil and simmer for 10 minutes. Blend in a liquidiser or food processor. Sieve. Taste and adjust seasoning if necessary. Flood the serving dish with yellow sauce. Ease the sides of the loaf tin with a sharp knife and turn out on to the sauce.

Garnish with sprigs of chervil.

25 g/1 oz butter
2 cloves garlic, crushed
225 g/8 oz leeks, trimmed, washed and finely chopped
salt and freshly ground black pepper
275 g/10 oz spinach, tough stalks discarded
50 g/2 oz fresh white breadcrumbs
2 eggs
1 egg yolk
pinch of grated nutmeg
350 ml/12 fl oz milk
2 yellow peppers, deseeded and roughly chopped
juice of $\frac{1}{2}$ lemon
1 shallot, finely chopped
150 ml/$\frac{1}{4}$ pint vegetable or chicken stock
sprigs of chervil to garnish

PROVENÇALE VEGETABLE SALAD

1 (50-g/2-oz) can anchovy fillets,
   drained
a little milk
½ yellow pepper
½ red pepper
½ green pepper
small bulb of fennel
½ cauliflower
225 g/8 oz broccoli
100 g/4 oz cap mushrooms, wiped
8 cherry tomatoes
100 g/4 oz English runner beans
6 tablespoons olive oil
3 tablespoons red wine vinegar
½ teaspoon fresh thyme leaves
1 tablespoon chopped fresh basil
1 tablespoon Dijon mustard
salt and freshly ground black pepper

A raw version of this recipe is seen on many a Provençale menu.

Serve in a large wooden salad bowl, tossed warm in the famous anchovy dressing. Every single vegetable in the world can be used for this recipe, so choose away! Serve with crusty brown bread and butter.

► Soak the anchovies in a little milk for 30 minutes. Drain and rinse in cold water. Deseed the peppers and cut into matchsticks. Cut the fennel into chunks and the cauliflower and broccoli into big florets. Top, tail and cut the runner beans in half. Wash the vegetables and steam over boiling water for 3–5 minutes.

Meanwhile make the dressing. Place the anchovies, oil, vinegar, thyme, basil and mustard in a liquidiser or food processor. Blend for a few seconds. Season well with salt and black pepper.

Toss the warm vegetables with the dressing and serve immediately.

GARDEN BEANS

During the summer months all of the vegetables are ready for harvesting at about the same time. This dish is perfect for combining two of these delicious crops in a creamy herb hollandaise.

▶ Season the beans with salt and black pepper. Toss in the lemon juice. Cover and steam over boiling water for 5–7 minutes or until just tender.

Meanwhile make the hollandaise sauce. Place the egg yolks and lemon juice in the liquidiser or food processor and season well with salt and pepper. Blend for a few seconds. With the machine running, gradually add the melted butter until the sauce is thick and light. Stir in the herbs. Taste and adjust seasoning if necessary.

Place the beans in a heated serving dish, spoon over the sauce and serve at once.

450 g/1 lb podded broad beans
450 g/1 lb French beans, topped and
  tailed and cut into quarters
salt and freshly ground black pepper
juice of $\frac{1}{2}$ lemon
Herb hollandaise
2 egg yolks
2 tablespoons lemon juice
salt and freshly ground black pepper
100 g/4 oz butter, melted
2 tablespoons chopped fresh herbs,
  for example, mint, parsley, dill,
  tarragon

CUCUMBER WITH FRESH PEAS AND MINT

1 cucumber
100 g/4 oz podded fresh peas (frozen will do perfectly well)
1 teaspoon lemon juice
1 teaspoon chopped mint
1 teaspoon sugar
25 g/1 oz butter
salt and freshly ground black pepper
sprigs of mint to garnish

A pretty garnish and vegetable accompaniment for steamed salmon. Perfect for that hot summer day!

▶ Rinse the cucumber and cut it into matchsticks. Cut a piece of foil large enough to seal the vegetables. Mix all ingredients together lightly. Pile on to the foil, season well with salt and pepper. Seal completely and steam over boiling water for 8 minutes.

Remove from the foil and garnish with sprigs of mint. Serve at once.

JUNE PEAS

1 kg/2 lb podded fresh peas (use frozen if necessary)
bunch of spring onions, trimmed and sliced
8 cos lettuce leaves, washed and shredded
2–3 sprigs of mint
1 tablespoon chopped parsley
1 teaspoon caster sugar
25 g/1 oz butter
1 clove garlic, crushed
salt and freshly ground black pepper

If you have a vegetable garden you will know that peas, spring onions and lettuce are all ready for picking in June. What better than to mix them together with fresh mint and serve with fish, poultry or game.

▶ Place a piece of wet greaseproof paper on the base of the steaming compartment. Top with peas, spring onions, lettuce, mint, parsley, sugar, butter and garlic. Season well with salt and freshly ground black pepper.

Cover with a tight fitting lid and steam over boiling water for 1 hour. *Check the liquid level frequently and add more boiling water if necessary.*

Check that the peas are tender; if they are, serve at once.

⫻ FOOD FACTS

▶ The garden pea has declined in popularity and become less a seasonal favourite since the advent of the excellent frozen alternative. Those with vegetable gardens and allotments continue to cultivate them but their early summer appearance in greengrocers is uncertain. When you do see them, they really are worth buying and preparing.

Peas should not be picked too large or they will be tough; plumpness and a bright green hue are the characteristics to look for. Taste and texture change after picking, when a process of converting sugar content to starch begins, so freshness is of the utmost importance.

CHICORY WITH FRESH PARMESAN

Crisp heads of chicory steamed with tomatoes and onions make a delicious vegetable accompaniment to meat or poultry. Vegetarians can double the recipe and serve with crusty bread.

▶ Remove the core from each piece of chicory. Brush with 1 teaspoon of lemon juice. Heat the butter in a pan. Fry the onion, garlic and tomatoes for 3 minutes. Season well with salt and black pepper.

Lay a piece of wet greaseproof paper in the steamer; arrange the spinach in an even layer on the top. Top with chicory and spoon on to the tomato and onion. Cover with a tight fitting lid and steam for 8 minutes.

Transfer to a warmed serving dish, sprinkle with Parmesan and serve at once.

4 heads of chicory, cut in half lengthways
1 teaspoon lemon juice
15 g/½ oz butter
2 onions, finely sliced
1 large clove garlic, crushed
4 tomatoes, peeled and deseeded
salt and freshly ground black pepper
100 g/4 oz spinach, stalks discarded
50 g/2 oz Parmesan cheese, freshly grated

FRESH VEGETABLE MOUNTAIN

This is a vegetable terrine that is not too difficult to prepare and is stunning to look at. Use half the quantity of the ingredients in the recipe to serve as a first course with herb vinaigrette, or use all the recipe as a vegetarian main course with baked potatoes, topped with chives and soured cream.

▶ Lightly oil a 1.15-litre/2-pint pudding basin. Drain inverted on absorbent kitchen paper. Steam the parsnips and carrots separately until soft.

Arrange the parsley leaves on the base of the pudding basin. Blend the parsnip in a liquidiser or food processor with one lot of egg and cream until smooth. Season with nutmeg, salt and pepper. Blend the carrot with egg and cream, seasoning with coriander, salt and pepper. Beat the remaining egg and cream into the spinach until smooth and creamy and season with nutmeg, salt and pepper.

Spoon the parsnip mixture into the base of the pudding basin. Top with a layer of carrot and finish with a smooth layer of spinach. Cover with foil or greaseproof paper and tie down with string. Place in a steamer or covered saucepan half-filled with boiling water and steam for 1 hour or until the mousse is firm to the touch.

To serve, run a knife around the sides of the mousse and turn out on to a plate. Serve hot or cold.

Parsnip layer
225 g/8 oz parsnips, peeled and roughly chopped
16 flat-leaf parsley leaves
1 large egg
50 ml/2 fl oz double cream
generous pinch of grated nutmeg
salt and freshly ground black pepper
Carrot layer
225 g/8 oz carrots, roughly chopped
1 large egg
50 ml/2 fl oz double cream
generous pinch of ground coriander
Spinach layer
1 large egg
50 ml/2 fl oz double cream
450 g/1 lb chopped frozen spinach, defrosted and dried thoroughly
generous pinch of grated nutmeg

STUFFED TOMATOES WITH GOAT'S CHEESE AND SORREL

8 ripe tomatoes
salt and freshly ground black pepper
4 large cos lettuce leaves, stalks
  discarded, shredded
100 g/4 oz goat's cheese, rind
  removed, finely chopped
2 shallots, finely chopped
1 tablespoon strips of fresh sorrel

For a vegetarian main course stuff with a mixture of fresh seasonal vegetables and herbs, serve with a light watercress sauce and crusty brown bread. The thought alone makes me feel hungry! For this recipe use basil if sorrel is not available.

▶ Slice open the stalk end of each tomato. Scoop out the seeds with a teaspoon and dry with absorbent kitchen paper. Season the insides of each with salt and freshly ground black pepper.

Mix the lettuce, cheese, shallot and sorrel. Season the mixture with salt and freshly ground black pepper.

Carefully fill the tomatoes. Place in the steamer. Cover with a tightly fitting lid and steam over boiling water for 6–8 minutes.

Serve at once.

WHOLE BEETROOT LACED WITH ORANGE

Beetroot is available throughout the year, and its colour can be put to particularly good effect in your meal planning, perhaps to perk up a dish. Fortunately for us it tastes excellent too!

▶ Place the beetroot in the steamer. Cover with a tight fitting lid and steam over boiling orange juice, half of the blanched rind, the vinegar and honey, for 20 minutes. *Check the liquid level frequently and add more boiling orange juice if necessary.*

Leave the beetroot to cool slightly whilst finishing the sauce. Boil to reduce until syrupy. Peel the beetroot and discard the skin. Slice on to serving plates and spoon over the sauce. Sprinkle with the remaining needleshreds.

Serve hot or cold.

12 baby beetroot, washed
300 ml/½ pint orange juice
pared rind of 1 orange, cut into thin needleshreds, and blanched for 20 seconds
2 tablespoons red wine vinegar
1 teaspoon honey
lemon wedges and coriander sprigs to garnish (optional)

CAULIFLOWER WITH TARRAGON TOMATO SAUCE

1 tablespoon olive oil
2 shallots, finely chopped
2 cloves garlic, crushed
2 (400-g/14-oz) cans chopped
    tomatoes in natural juice
25 g/1 oz sugar
2 tablespoons tarragon vinegar
1 tablespoon chopped fresh
    tarragon
salt and freshly ground black pepper
1 large cauliflower
chopped fresh tarragon to garnish

For a vegetarian main course serve with bean salad and crusty brown bread, or mix with broccoli florets for a colourful alternative.

▶ Heat the oil in a pan, fry the shallot and garlic for 2 minutes. Stir in the tomatoes, sugar, vinegar and tarragon. Season with salt and black pepper. Bring to the boil and simmer for 2 minutes.

Wash the cauliflower and cut into quarters. Place in a suitable bowl, and season with salt and pepper. Pour over the sauce. Cover with foil and greaseproof paper and tie down. Place in a steamer or covered saucepan half-filled with boiling water and steam for 25 minutes. *Check the liquid level frequently and add more boiling water if necessary.*

Remove the paper or tin foil and serve at once, sprinkled with chopped fresh tarragon. SERVES 4–6.

PEPPER POTS

4 yellow, green or red peppers
salt and freshly ground black pepper
1 tablespoon olive oil
50 g/2 oz rindless smoked bacon,
    diced
4 spring onions, trimmed and sliced
175 g/6 oz podded broad beans
100 g/4 oz broccoli florets, roughly
    chopped
100 g/4 oz cottage cheese
7 g/¼ oz fresh horseradish, grated
    (use ½ tablespoon horseradish
    sauce if necessary)
1 tablespoon chopped parsley

A cage of summer vegetables. Peppers are available all year round so in the winter they could be stuffed with Brussels sprouts and leeks. For a main course, double the recipe and serve with lightly dressed salad. Vegetarians can omit the bacon.

▶ Slice the top off the peppers, deseed, and rinse under cold water. Season the insides of the peppers with salt and pepper. Heat the oil in a pan. Gently fry the bacon and spring onion for 3 minutes. Stir in the beans and broccoli, cook for 2 minutes. Stir in the cottage cheese, horseradish and parsley. Season with salt and pepper.

Spoon the mixture into the pepper shells and place in the steamer. Cover with a tightly fitting lid and steam over boiling water for 10 minutes.

Serve the pepper pots whole on warmed plates or slice open to show the creamy filling. Eat immediately.

AVOCADO POPOVERS

A delicate mixture of avocado strips, smoked ham, and spring onions wrapped tightly in lettuce leaves and served with a sharp lemon sauce. This can be served as a light and unusual first course or a pretty vegetable accompaniment for fish and chicken. The popovers can be served with or without the sauce.

▶ Steam the lettuce leaves over boiling water for 15–20 seconds. Refresh in ice-cold water.

Mix the avocado, lemon juice, ham, and spring onion in a bowl. Season with salt and pepper. Divide the avocado mixture between each lettuce leaf and wrap tightly. Lay side by side in the steamer. Cover with a tight fitting lid and steam over boiling water for 5 minutes.

Meanwhile make the sauce. Place the egg yolks and lemon juice in a liquidiser or food processor. Season well with salt and pepper and blend for a few seconds. With the machine running, gradually add the melted butter until the sauce is thick and light. Taste and adjust seasoning if necessary.

Flood the base of four individual plates with the sauce. Top with the avocado popovers. Garnish with the lemon rind and serve at once.

8 lettuce leaves
1 large avocado, peeled and cut
   into strips
juice of 1 lemon
2 slices smoked ham, cut into strips
bunch of spring onions, trimmed
   and finely sliced
salt and freshly ground black pepper
pared rind of $\frac{1}{4}$ lemon, cut into thin
   strips and blanched for garnish
Lemon sauce
3 egg yolks
3 tablespoons lemon juice
salt and freshly ground black pepper
100 g/4 oz unsalted butter, melted

HONEY-GLAZED PARSNIPS

▶ Brush the parsnips with the honey. Coat them evenly in toasted sesame seeds and season well with salt and pepper.

Place in a steamer and cover with a tight-fitting lid. Steam over the boiling stock or water for 20 minutes or until tender. Keep hot, or serve immediately.

8 baby parsnips, peeled and
   trimmed
1 tablespoon clear honey, warmed
3 tablespoons toasted sesame seeds
salt and freshly ground black pepper
450 ml/$\frac{3}{4}$ pint vegetable stock or
   water

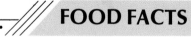 **FOOD FACTS**

▶ Of tropical American origin, avocados are now widely cultivated in hot countries for their rich nutritional content.

Strictly speaking, the avocado is a fruit, but features most commonly in a savoury context; however, as a starter, it often shares a successful fruity alliance sliced alternately with grapefruit or mango and dressed with a good vinaigrette.

If avocados are slightly under-ripe when you buy them, then leave them in a warm place and in two or three days they should be ready for eating. Avocados give slightly to the touch when ripe.

A disadvantage when preparing avocados in advance is that they discolour when cut. A sprinkling of lemon juice or other citrus juice will prevent short-term discolouration.

To halve an avocado, cut downwards with a sharp knife from the stalk, cutting right round the stone, then gently pull the two halves apart, and remove the stone.

If slicing, peel each half, place on a work surface, cut-side down, and slice in from the stalk end downwards. Avocado circles and rings can be achieved by leaving the avocado whole, peeling it, then slicing across, negotiating the stone carefully when the knife hits it.

A TASTE OF TRADITION

A book on steamed food would not be complete without the traditional recipes that we all love so much. Believe it or not, the recipe for Steak and Kidney Pudding – so famous among England's national dishes that you would think I should have essays to write about its history – was written down for the first time as late as 1840.

The majority of chapters concentrate on a healthy approach to eating; however, there is nothing wrong with nutritious full-flavoured and traditional foods like good old British suet pudding that we all crave for from time to time. By all means treat yourself occasionally but I wouldn't advise eating this type of food for every meal! Suet and meat puddings as well as traditional casseroles are foods that require prolonged and gentle cooking. In this chapter I have included all of these cooked by steaming: the puddings would probably be steamed anyway, but casseroles are normally baked in the oven. Once again, you will no longer have to put up with stringy meat in your casserole!

Jam Roly Poly (page 76)

KENTISH CHICKEN PUDDING

This is one of many puddings that Kent and East Sussex are famous for. You will need a good appetite for this filling traditional peasant dish which was ideal for the very poor who could have a hot two-course meal by boiling the pudding and meat together in the same pot.

▶ Make the suet crust pastry. Place the flour, salt and suet in a food processor. Process for a couple of seconds to mix thoroughly. Add enough water to mix to a soft dough. Do not process for too long as the pastry will be tough.

Roll out the pastry to a thickness of about 1 cm/$\frac{1}{2}$ in. Grease a 1.4-litre/$2\frac{1}{2}$-pint pudding basin and line with the pastry, reserving enough to make the lid. In lining the basin and sealing the pastry lid, follow the instructions given for Steak and Kidney Pudding on page 66.

Mix together the chicken, pork, onion, apple and herbs, season well with salt and pepper. Pile in to within 2.5 cm/1 in of the top of the pudding basin. Add the chicken stock or water to the meat. Roll out the remaining pastry and cover the pudding with it.

Cover with greased foil or greaseproof paper. Tie down with string. Lower the basin into a pan of boiling water (the water should only come halfway up the basin). Cover with a tight fitting lid and steam for $2\frac{1}{2}$ hours. *Check the liquid level frequently and add more boiling water if necessary.*

Remove the foil and serve straight from the bowl.

350 g/12 oz self-raising flour, sifted
pinch of salt
175 g/6 oz shredded beef suet
water to mix
1.25 kg/$2\frac{1}{2}$ lb boneless chicken, cut into bite-sized pieces
225 g/8 oz salt belly pork, cut into bite-sized pieces
2 small onions, finely chopped
2 large cooking apples, peeled, cored and chopped
2 tablespoons chopped fresh herbs, for example, parsley, thyme, chives, tarragon
salt and freshly ground black pepper
3 tablespoons chicken stock or water

NEW WAVE COQ AU VIN

This is one of France's most famous dishes. There are millions of recipes for coq au vin and the one below is my favourite. Steaming this dish might seem a little unusual, but the results are always succulent and tender.

▶ Dust the chicken pieces with the flour and season well with salt and pepper. Heat the oil in a heavy-based pan and fry the joints over a high heat until golden brown on all sides. Remove from the pan. Fry the bacon, garlic and onions for 2 minutes. Add the mushrooms and continue cooking for 2 minutes. Return the chicken to the pan. Turn off the heat. Warm the brandy in a spoon, set light to it and pour flaming over the chicken. As soon as the flames subside, pour in the wine and stock. Bring to the boil, scraping any sediment from the base of the pan. Pour the contents of the pan into a suitable dish. Season well with salt, pepper and the thyme. Cover with a piece of foil and tie down with string.

Place in a steamer or covered saucepan half-filled with boiling water, and steam for 45 minutes. Remove the pudding basin and then the foil. Pour the cooking liquid into an empty saucepan and bring to the boil. Boil the liquid to reduce until syrupy. Spoon over the chicken and sprinkle with chopped parsley. Arrange the croûtons on top and serve at once.

1 (1.5-kg/3-lb) chicken, jointed into eight pieces
15 g/$\frac{1}{2}$ oz plain flour
salt and freshly ground pepper
2 tablespoons olive oil
150 g/5 oz rindless streaky bacon, diced
2 cloves garlic, finely chopped
12 button onions
12 button mushrooms, wiped
2 tablespoons brandy
150 ml/$\frac{1}{4}$ pint red wine
300 ml/$\frac{1}{2}$ pint chicken stock
$\frac{1}{4}$ teaspoon chopped fresh thyme
Garnish
2 tablespoons chopped parsley
triangular bread croûtons

SPRING CHICKENS WITH FRESH PARSLEY SAUCE

2 (1-kg/2-lb) spring chickens, or 1 (1.75-kg/4-lb) chicken, giblets reserved
salt and freshly ground black pepper
1 shallot, finely sliced
2 small carrots, roughly chopped
1 leek, trimmed, washed and sliced
6 peppercorns
1 bay leaf
300 ml/½ pint white wine
2 parsley sprigs
1.15 litres/2 pints water
Parsley sauce
25 g/1 oz butter
25 g/1 oz plain flour
300 ml/½ pint milk
4 tablespoons chopped parsley

Parsley was the essential ingredient for the famous medieval 'green sauce', a herb sauce that used to be the appropriate accompaniment for chicken or fish.
It is an easily digestible dish, so both good for those that are unwell and also a sound meal for the healthy!
Tarragon is a good alternative to parsley if preferred.

▶ Wipe the chicken(s) and season well with salt and black pepper. Put the giblets in a saucepan with the vegetables, peppercorns, bay leaf, wine and parsley. Add the water. Bring to the boil. Put the chicken(s) in a steamer, cover with a tight fitting lid and steam gently over the giblet stock for 1½ hours. *Check the liquid level frequently and add more boiling water if necessary.*

When the chicken(s) are cooked, remove the skin and keep warm. Strain the stock into a clean pan and discard the giblets and vegetables. Bring to the boil and remove any scum from the surface.

Melt the butter in a separate saucepan over a gentle heat, add the flour and cook for 2 minutes stirring constantly. Remove from the heat and add 300 ml/½ pint of the stock and the milk. Bring to the boil and stir well until smooth and thickened. Add the parsley and taste to check seasoning. Adjust if necessary. Either spoon the sauce over the chicken to serve, or serve the sauce separately.

FOOD FACTS

▶ To bone a chicken, turn the bird with the breast down on a clean surface. Use a sharp knife to cut down the length of the back, then cut under the skin, working as close to the bone as possible and remove all the meat. Keep the skin in one piece and scrape the meat downwards off the bones or out of all the crannies. Take particular care when you reach the soft breast bone not to break the skin. Cut a very fine sliver of bone off to avoid this. Turn the chicken round and work the other side free from the bones.

GALANTINE OF CHICKEN WITH LEMON SAGE STUFFING

The word galantine means 'a mixture of cooked meats or poultry set in their own jelly and served cold'.

Galantine of chicken is one of the most famous and traditional English dishes. Get the butcher to bone the chicken but keep the bones for the stock. You can use other flavoured stuffings if you wish.

▶ Place the sausage meat, ham, onion, sage, the lemon rind and juice, and the egg in a bowl and mix thoroughly. Season well with salt and black pepper. Lay the chicken on a board, skin side down. Season all over with salt and pepper. With a knife spread the stuffing mixture on the chicken to within 1 cm/½ in of the edges. Draw the sides of the chicken over the stuffing to reshape and sew neatly together with fine string. Place in a steamer.

Cover with a tight fitting lid and steam over the chicken stock for about 1½ hours. (Time permitting, you can always steam the chicken over the ingredients for the stock. Remember you will have to increase the time for reducing the liquid to make the glaze.) *Check the liquid level frequently and add more boiling stock if necessary.* When cooked, press the chicken parcel between two plates with a heavy weight on top. Leave until cold. Remove the sewing thread.

Meanwhile, strain the stock and boil rapidly to reduce. Allow to cool.

Arrange the garnish on top of the galantine and glaze with the reduced stock. Serve cold. SERVES 6

225 g/8 oz sausage meat
100 g/4 oz lean cooked ham, finely chopped
1 large onion, finely chopped
8 sage leaves, finely chopped or 1 teaspoon rubbed sage
grated rind and juice of 1½ lemons
1 egg, beaten
salt and freshly ground black pepper
1 (1.75-kg/4-lb) chicken, boned and wiped
600 ml/1 pint boiling chicken stock (page 36)
Garnish
lemon slices
fresh sage leaves

QUEEN'S CORONATION CHICKEN

A popular summer dish that was devised by the Cordon Bleu School for the coronation celebrations in 1953.

▶ Wipe the chicken and season with lemon juice, salt and pepper. Place in a steamer. Cover with a tight fitting lid and steam over the stock for 1½ hours. *Check the liquid level frequently and add more boiling stock or water if necessary.* Let the chicken get cold.

Meanwhile make the sauce. Mix together all remaining ingredients and stir in enough milk to make a smooth coating consistency.

Remove the meat from the chicken bones and when cold, mix with the sauce reserving a small quantity.

Pile the chicken into the middle of a serving dish and coat with the remaining sauce. Garnish with watercress and serve with wild rice salad, if liked. The photograph on page 62 shows an attractive serving suggestion. SERVES 4–6

1 (1.75-kg/4-lb) chicken, giblets removed
1 teaspoon lemon juice
salt and freshly ground black pepper
600 ml/1 pint boiling chicken stock (page 36)
300 ml/½ pint mayonnaise
2 teaspoons apricot jam, sieved
½ teaspoon tomato purée
2 teaspoons curry powder
2 tablespoons fromage frais
milk
watercress sprigs to garnish

POUSSIN WITH SCOTTISH EGG SAUCE

This was apparently Mary, Queen of Scots' favourite sauce. It is a clever combination of eggs and milk and goes beautifully with fish as well as chicken.

Wipe the poussin, season well with salt, white pepper and lemon juice. Sprinkle with chives and place in the steamer. Cover with a tight fitting lid and steam over the chicken stock for 45 minutes.

Meanwhile heat the milk, bay leaf, white peppercorns and chives over a gentle heat for a few minutes. Cover and leave to one side to infuse for 15 minutes. Strain. When the poussin are cooked transfer to a warmed serving dish and keep warm. Melt the butter over gentle heat, stir in the flour and cook for 3 minutes.

Mix the strained milk and remaining stock in a measuring jug and add water if necessary to make the amount up to 600 ml/1 pint. Lower the heat and add the liquid to the butter and flour. Bring to the boil and simmer for 3 minutes, stirring continuously until the sauce thickens. Stir in the chopped eggs. Season well with salt and white pepper.

Spoon the sauce over the poussin and garnish with chopped chives, or serve separately in a sauce boat.

4 (350-g/12-oz) poussin
salt and freshly ground white pepper
2 teaspoons lemon juice
1 tablespoon chopped chives
600 ml/1 pint boiling chicken stock
chopped chives to garnish
Egg sauce
300 ml/½ pint milk
1 bay leaf
4 white peppercorns
2 tablespoons chopped chives
25 g/1 oz butter
25 g/1 oz plain flour
2 hard-boiled eggs, finely chopped

GAMMON WITH APPLE

This medieval method of cooking sweet and savoury tastes started in Shropshire. A version of this dish was often nicknamed 'Fidget Pie' and was traditionally served to the farmers during harvest as a hearty evening meal.

Soak the gammon cuts in cold water for at least 2 hours before cooking, to remove any excess salt. If you do not have the time then the quickest way is to cover the meat with cold water, bring to the boil, then drain and replace the water before cooking.

▶ Layer the potatoes, gammon, onion, garlic, turnip, carrot and apple in a bowl, seasoning with salt, pepper, sage and thyme as you go.

Pour over enough stock to just cover the filling. Cover the bowl with foil or greaseproof paper and tie down. Place in a steamer or covered saucepan half-filled with boiling water and steam for 1½ hours. *Check the liquid level frequently and add more boiling water if necessary.*

Remove the foil. Pour the cooking liquid carefully into a pan, leaving the meat and vegetables in the bowl. Keep the food warm to one side. Boil the sauce to reduce to half of the original volume. Taste and adjust seasoning if necessary. Pour the sauce over the food and garnish with sage and thyme.

675 g/1½ lb potatoes, peeled and thickly sliced
675 g/1½ lb gammon, soaked and cut into bite-sized pieces, rind and fat removed
1 large onion, sliced
1 clove garlic, crushed
2 turnips, peeled and quartered
2 carrots, thickly sliced
3 small cooking apples, peeled and thickly sliced
salt and freshly ground black pepper
½ teaspoon chopped fresh or ¼ teaspoon rubbed sage
¼ teaspoon chopped fresh or pinch of dried thyme
300 ml/½ pint chicken stock
sprigs of sage and thyme to garnish

*From the top: Queen's Coronation Chicken;
Galantine of Chicken with Lemon Sage Stuffing (page 61)*

LANCASHIRE HOT POT

2 joints best end neck of lamb, cut
    into cutlets
salt and freshly ground black pepper
1 kg/2 lb potatoes, peeled and
    thickly sliced
3 lamb's kidneys, skinned, cored and
    quartered
4 small carrots, quartered
2 onions, sliced
225 g/8 oz cap mushrooms, wiped
½ teaspoon chopped fresh thyme
2 tablespoons chopped parsley
300 ml/½ pint beef or chicken stock
chopped parsley to garnish

Lancashire hot pot was traditionally cooked in the old bread ovens. The proper recipe used mutton and oysters, but as both are fairly scarce now, lamb and mushrooms will have to do. Steaming a stew like this eliminates the problems of disintegrating food, as well as sealing in all the goodness and taste. Aim to serve two or three chops per person depending on your purse and their appetite!

▶ Trim the excess fat from the meat and season the cutlets with salt and black pepper. Place a layer of potatoes in the base of a large suitable bowl and season. Arrange the cutlets and kidney on top. Add the carrot, onion and mushrooms. Season to taste, then sprinkle with the thyme and parsley.

Finish with a neat layer of potatoes. Pour in the stock. Cover the bowl with foil and tie down with string. Place in a steamer or covered saucepan half-filled with boiling water and steam for 2 hours. *Check the liquid level frequently and add more boiling water if necessary.*

Remove the foil and sprinkle the hot pot with chopped parsley. Serve at once.

OLD ENGLISH MEAT LOAF

450 g/1 lb stewing steak or topside
    of beef, finely minced
350 g/12 oz rindless lean bacon,
    finely minced
100 g/4 oz lamb's liver, finely minced
1 onion, finely chopped
50 g/2 oz fresh white breadcrumbs
2 eggs, beaten
2 tablespoons chopped parsley
small pinch of dried thyme
2 teaspoons chopped fresh basil
salt and freshly ground black pepper

Meat loaf was originally invented in medieval times for keeping the trencherman's hunger at bay. My grandmother produces an outstanding version of this which works wonders on our own hunger every time. It is important to buy lean stewing beef or topside, and mince it finely yourself because ready-minced beef is usually too fatty and coarse for this recipe.

▶ Grease a 1.15-litre/2-pint pudding basin. Mix all of the ingredients together in a large mixing bowl. Season very well with salt and pepper. Pile the mixture into the pudding basin. Cover with foil or greaseproof paper and tie down with string.

Gently cook in a steamer or covered saucepan half-filled with boiling water, for 2 hours. *Check the liquid level frequently and add more boiling water if necessary.*

Cool the loaf in the pudding basin, pressing it down with weights. Slice the meat loaf and serve hot or cold. SERVES 4–6

SILVERSIDE WITH MUSTARD AND HERB DUMPLINGS

Silverside comes from the hind quarters of the beef. It is one of the tastiest but toughest joints, so cooking needs to be long and slow.

Dumplings were first made in Norfolk and eaten in large quantities during the cold winter months. They were originally made plain with suet but as people began to experiment, the variety of flavours and colours increased. The dumplings can be poached in the stock while the pot roast is cooking above.

▶ Place the meat on the vegetables in a steamer. Season well with salt and pepper. Cover with a tight fitting lid and steam over the stock for 2 hours. *Check the liquid level frequently and add more boiling·stock if necessary.*

Meanwhile, mix together all the ingredients for the dumplings, except the egg and prepared mustard, in a mixing bowl. Blend in the beaten egg. Lightly flour your hands and shape the mixture into balls the size of walnuts. Make a hole in each by pushing a finger into it. Put a small amount of mustard in each hole and squeeze the dough to seal it in tightly. Drop the dumplings into the stock and continue to steam the beef as before for 8 minutes. Turn the dumplings over and cook for a further 8 minutes.

To serve, arrange the joint and vegetables on a large serving dish surrounded with dumplings and keep warm.

Reduce the stock until rich and syrupy and pour over the meat. Garnish with sprigs of parsley, sage, majoram and thyme.

1.25 kg/2½ lb silverside of beef
2 carrots, diced
2 celery sticks, diced
2 onions, sliced
4 leeks, trimmed, washed and sliced
2 cloves garlic, crushed
salt and freshly ground black pepper
600 ml/1 pint boiling beef stock
sprigs of parsley, sage, majoram and thyme to garnish
Dumplings
50 g/2 oz self-raising flour
50 g/2 oz fresh white breadcrumbs
1 teaspoon mustard powder
40 g/1½ oz shredded suet
2 tablespoons chopped fresh herbs, for example, parsley, sage, marjoram, thyme
salt and freshly ground black pepper
1 egg, beaten
2 teaspoons prepared mustard

FOOD FACTS

▶ When well prepared, traditional savoury puddings represent the best in English regional food. The flavour of the ingredients locked into the suet crust and gently steamed is superb.

Interestingly, the medieval cook liberally combined sweet with savoury, which comes as a surprise to those accustomed to a strict division between flavours in a single dish. Fruits such as dates, prunes and raisins, spices like cloves, cinnamon and mace were mixed with meat such as mutton or beef

and, as well as these inclusions, it was suggested that lots of sugar was added too! This rather explains the various compositions of Christmas Pudding over the ages, detailed in my

introduction to the recipe on page 74.

Gradually, the sweet and savoury divide was established, although survivors featuring in this chapter are Kentish Chicken

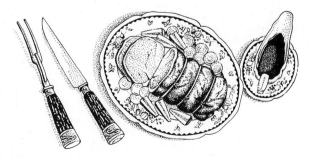

Pudding and Gammon with Apple.

An interesting anomoly, in view of their current status as luxury items, is that oysters were freely popped into Steak and Kidney Puddings by the Victorians because they were common fare at the time. The oyster beds became depleted at the end of the last century and they are obviously far too expensive to use now. If you do feel inclined to be extravagant you will find that oysters are rich in minerals, especially zinc.

STEAK AND KIDNEY PUDDING

350 g/12 oz self-raising flour
salt and freshly ground black pepper
175 g/6 oz shredded beef suet
water to mix
1 tablespoon plain flour
675 g/1½ lb chuck steak, cut into
   bite-sized pieces, fat removed
225 g/8 oz lamb's or ox kidney,
   cored, sinew removed and diced
1 onion, finely chopped
2 tablespoons chopped parsley
2–3 tablespoons beef stock or water

▶ Grease a 1.15–1.4-litre/2–2½-pint pudding basin with a little butter. Mix the self-raising flour, a pinch of salt, the suet and enough water to make a soft but not sticky dough. Reserving one-third of the quantity for a lid, roll out the pastry into a circle. Line the basin, easing the pastry when necessary to fit, and trimming the top to come 1 cm/½ in above the edge of the basin.

Season the plain flour well with salt and pepper and dip in the meat and kidney. Fill the lined basin with the meat, onion and parsley. Spoon on the stock or water. Roll out the remaining pastry to cover the pudding and dampen the edges. Put on the lid, dampened edges upwards, and fold over the pastry rim, pressing down lightly to seal. Cover the top of the basin with pleated foil or greaseproof paper and tie down well with string. Place in a steamer or covered saucepan half-filled with boiling water and steam for 4 hours. *Check the liquid level frequently and add boiling water if necessary.*

Serve the pudding in the basin with a clean napkin or tea-towel pinned round it.

FAMILY POT ROAST

Pot roasting is one of the oldest methods of cooking, dating back to prehistoric days. Choose a joint of beef that has little fat, such as topside or silverside, which require slow gentle cooking.

▶ Heat the oil in a heavy-based pan. Season the beef with salt and pepper. Fry the beef until golden brown on all sides. Remove from the pan and put to one side. Pour the stock and wine into the same pan. Bring to the boil, scraping the sediment from the base of the pan. Pour into a clean saucepan. Bring to the boil.

Arrange the vegetables, thyme and garlic in the steamer and season to taste. Place the joint of beef on top. Cover the steamer with a tight fitting lid and steam over the boiling stock for 1 hour 45 minutes. *Check the liquid level frequently and add more boiling stock if necessary.* Throw in the mushrooms, and continue cooking the beef for a further 20 minutes. Serve the meat on a warmed dish surrounded by the vegetables. Remove the pan from the heat and skim off all fat from the surface of the stock, then boil to reduce until syrupy and serve separately.

2 tablespoons olive oil or beef dripping
1.5 kg/3 lb topside or silverside of beef, rolled and tied
salt and freshly ground black pepper
900 ml/1½ pint beef stock
150 ml/¼ pint red wine
2 onions, quartered
8 small carrots
8 small turnips, peeled
1 small swede, peeled and cubed
1 teaspoon chopped fresh or ¼ teaspoon dried thyme
4 cloves garlic, crushed
450 g/1 lb cap mushrooms, wiped

'LOVE-IN-DISGUISE'

4 small lamb's hearts
50 g/2 oz pork sausage meat
50 g/2 oz rindless smoked bacon
½ teaspoon chopped fresh or ¼
  teaspoon rubbed sage
1 tablespoon chopped parsley
½ onion, finely chopped
1 clove garlic, crushed
2 teaspoons tomato purée
1 egg yolk, beaten
25 g/1 oz fresh white breadcrumbs
salt and freshly ground black pepper
15 g/½ oz plain flour
1 tablespoon olive oil
450 ml/¾ pint beef or lamb stock
sprigs of sage to garnish

This name was given to stuffed hearts in Tudor times. Try this recipe for a cheap and nourishing evening meal, and serve it with buttered mashed potatoes. Buy lamb's hearts if possible as they are more tender; if not, ox or calf's hearts will do just as well.

Be patient because they need long, slow cooking to tenderise but they are well worth the wait.

▶ Soak the hearts in slightly salted water for 1 hour changing the water every 15 minutes. Cut away the lobes and white membrane and remove any blood from the cavity. Dry the hearts on absorbent kitchen paper.

Place the sausage meat, bacon, sage, parsley, onion, garlic, tomato purée, egg and breadcrumbs in a liquidiser or food processor. Blend until the ingredients are finely minced. Season well with salt and black pepper. Fill each heart with the stuffing, fold over the flap at the top and secure with a skewer. Season the flour with salt and pepper and dip in the stuffed hearts. Heat the oil in a heavy-based pan and fry them until golden brown on all sides. Transfer to a pudding basin. Pour the stock into the frying pan. Bring to the boil scraping the sediment from the base of the pan. Pour over the hearts. Cover with foil or greaseproof paper and tie down well with string. Gently cook in a steamer or covered saucepan, half filled with water, for 2–2½ hours. *Check liquid level frequently and add more boiling water if necessary.*

Remove the paper and arrange the hearts on a warmed serving dish and keep warm. Tip the stock into a clean pan and boil rapidly to reduce until rich and syrupy. Pour over the hearts and garnish with sprigs of sage.

FOOD FACTS

▶ The word offal is composed of two words, 'off-fall', or the off-cuts from a carcass. The reputation of these meats has been variable over the ages, but offal's valuable contribution to a healthy diet is now fully recognised.

With careful preparation and cooking, offal can be delicious. Low in fat and rich in vitamins and minerals, it is a worthwhile introduction into the diet if you haven't already made a point of including it.

Sadly it is the preparation of offal that is off-putting to many people, mainly because they are unsure of exactly how to approach the task. The following notes may be of some help if you are not confident.

Heart is a food that needs lengthy cooking. Once the outer fat, membranes, pipes and all tendons have been removed the hearts should be rinsed and dried.

Tongue is available either fresh or pickled in brine. Before cooking it should be soaked for several hours in cold water if pickled or in a brine solution if fresh. The cooked tongue must have all skin and bone (root) removed along with any fat and gristle. It can then be served hot or rolled and pressed for cold presentation.

Oxtail has an excellent flavour and needs little preparation since it is usually sold jointed ready for use. Once trimmed of fat it needs lengthy cooking to yield a tender and full-flavoured result.

STEAMED OXTAIL CASSEROLE

Oxen were useful animals to the ancient Celts, as they worked on the land hauling the heavy ploughs through the fields. For the farmer the ultimate advantage was that the animal could be eaten when its working life was over! Like all other parts of the oxen, oxtail needs to be cooked very slowly but the taste is well worth waiting for. Oxtail is inexpensive and usually sold nowadays ready skinned and in portions.

▶ Heat the oil in a heavy-based pan. Season the flour and dip in the oxtail, then fry over high heat until golden brown on all sides. Transfer to a pudding basin. Fry the vegetables for 5 minutes. Spoon over the meat. Stir in the herbs and cloves. Season well.

Pour the stock into the frying pan. Bring to the boil scraping the sediment from the base of the pan. Pour over the meat and vegetables. Cover with a piece of foil or greaseproof paper and tie down with string. Place in a steamer or covered saucepan, half-filled with boiling water and steam for $3\frac{1}{2}$ hours. *Check the liquid level frequently and add more boiling water when necessary.*

Arrange the oxtail on a warmed serving dish and keep warm. Blend the vegetables and stock in a liquidiser or food processor. Spoon over the meat, sprinkle with chopped parsley and serve at once.

2 tablespoons oil
salt and freshly ground black pepper
15 g/$\frac{1}{4}$ oz plain flour
1 medium oxtail, jointed
2 medium onions, sliced
4 carrots, thinly sliced
2 leeks, trimmed, washed and sliced
2 cloves garlic, crushed
2 large turnips, peeled and roughly
  chopped
pinch of dried thyme
2 bay leaves
pinch of rubbed sage
small pinch of ground cloves
450 ml/$\frac{3}{4}$ pint beef stock
2 tablespoons chopped parsley to
  garnish

OX TONGUE

Ox tongue was for a long time the only type of offal to be served at a gentleman's table. It can be served hot in its natural shape with Cumberland, tomato or mustard sauce, or served cold, rolled and set in jellied stock, and eaten with salads. The traditional recipe involves boiling the tongue. The stock that is made is both greasy and tasteless and is normally discarded. The way to retain all the great nutritional benefits from fresh tongue, without boiling them away, is to steam gently.

▶ Soak the tongue in cold water for 2 hours. Drain and season it with salt and black pepper. Sprinkle with chopped herbs. Arrange the vegetables in the steamer and top with the tongue. Cover with a tight fitting lid and steam over the stock for 3 hours. *Check the liquid level frequently and add more boiling stock if necessary.*

When cooked, lift the tongue on to a board, remove the bones at the root and the skin. Discard the vegetables. Serve hot with mustard sauce. To serve cold, curl the cooked tongue into a large round cake tin or soufflé dish. Make the stock up to 600 ml/1 pint using water or additional stock. Dissolve the gelatine in the stock, and pour over the tongue. Cover with foil and place a heavy weight on the meat.

Refrigerate overnight. To serve, turn out, and carve thin round slices. Serve with salads.

1 (1.5–1.6-kg/3–$3\frac{1}{2}$-lb) ox tongue
salt and freshly ground black pepper
2 tablespoons chopped fresh herbs,
  for example, thyme, parsley,
  chervil, sage
1 large carrot, cut into matchsticks
1 large onion, sliced
2 small turnips, peeled and sliced
2 celery sticks, sliced
900 ml/$1\frac{1}{2}$ pints beef stock
15 g/$\frac{1}{2}$ oz gelatine

OXFORD VENISON

For those of you that were or are, students of Magdalen College, Oxford, there is one dish that you will undoubtedly know.

Oxford Venison has been served at the college for two and a half centuries at the yearly Restoration Dinner.

It was originally a saddle of venison from the college's own herd, marinated for days, braised in red wine and glazed with chestnuts.

My version follows the principles of the centuries-old recipe, except that, however hard you push, a saddle of venison will not fit into a steamer; so I will be using steaks!!

▶ Season the steaks with salt and pepper. Lie them in a dish with the onion, carrot, red wine, thyme, bay leaves, garlic, peppercorns, juniper berries and half of the oil.

Leave to marinate for at least 24 hours, turning occasionally. The longer the meat is allowed to marinate the more gamey the flavour. Drain and reserve the marinade, drying the steaks on absorbent kitchen paper. Cut a piece of foil large enough to seal all of the ingredients completely.

Heat the butter and remaining oil in a heavy-based pan. Fry the steaks over high heat until golden brown on all sides, add the onions, mushrooms and chestnuts and fry for 3 minutes.

Lay the browned steaks and vegetables in the middle of the foil. Fold up the edges to avoid any juices escaping. Boil the juices of the marinade to half of the original quantity and strain the sauce over the venison. Pour in the port and redcurrant jelly. Season once more with salt and pepper. Seal the foil parcel completely. Steam gently over boiling water for 45 minutes. *Check the liquid level frequently and add more boiling water if necessary.*

Arrange the venison and vegetables on warmed serving plates and keep warm. Boil the wine mixture to reduce until rich and syrupy. Pour over the food and garnish with sprigs of parsley and thyme.

4 (275-g/10-oz) venison steaks
salt and freshly ground black pepper
1 onion, finely sliced
1 carrot, finely sliced
300 ml/$\frac{1}{2}$ pint red wine
sprig of thyme
2 bay leaves
1 clove garlic, crushed
black peppercorns
2 juniper berries, crushed (optional)
2 tablespoons olive oil
25 g/1 oz butter
12 button onions
12 button mushrooms
1 (200-g/7-oz) can whole chestnuts
   in water
150 ml/$\frac{1}{4}$ pint port
1 tablespoon redcurrant jelly
sprigs of parsley and thyme to
   garnish

*From the top: Ox Tongue (page 69);
Oxford Venison (this page)*

SAVOURY STUFFED MARROW

225 g/8 oz lean beef, minced
1 onion, finely chopped
1 clove garlic, finely chopped
1 green pepper, deseeded and finely
    chopped
150 ml/¼ pint beef stock
3 tablespoons red wine
1 tablespoon tomato purée
2 teaspoons chopped fresh basil
1 tablespoon chopped parsley
salt and freshly ground black pepper
1 marrow, peeled, cut in half
    lengthways and deseeded
50 g/2 oz cheese, grated, to garnish

Choose young marrows, no longer than 30 cm/12 in. Avoid older ones as they have coarse flesh and tough skins.

Stuff with the filling below, or use a similar quantity of any other meat or vegetable mixture.

▶ Heat a frying pan and fry the mince, onion, garlic and green pepper until golden brown. Stir in the stock, wine, tomato purée, basil and parsley. Season well with salt and black pepper.

Bring to the boil and simmer for 10 minutes. Cut a piece of foil large enough to completely seal the marrow. Season the insides of the marrow and spoon in the meat mixture. Wrap tightly to seal completely. Place in a steamer, cover with a tight fitting lid and steam over boiling water for 20 minutes. *Check the liquid level frequently and add more boiling water if necessary.* Remove the foil and lift the stuffed marrow on to a warmed serving plate, sprinkle with cheese and serve at once.

STEAMED NETTLES

675 g/1½ lb young nettle leaves,
    stalks discarded
juice of 1 lemon
salt and freshly ground black pepper
25 g/1 oz butter

▶ Wash the nettles and remove any old leaves.

Place in the steamer. Sprinkle with lemon juice, salt and pepper. Cover with a tight fitting lid and steam over boiling water for 10 minutes.

Melt the butter in a pan. Add the nettles and toss to coat them thoroughly in butter. Serve at once.

Another famous traditional vegetable is the samphire or sea fennel, a fleshy plant that can be found amongst cliffs, rocky coasts and marshlands. If you are lucky enough to find it, then you can cook it in the same way as the nettles.

▶ There was a time, some of us may reflect with nostalgia, when a steamed pudding was a regular item on the family menu. With the advantages of cheapness and a capacity for incorporating a great variety of store-cupboard items and transforming them into mouth-watering and satisfying concoctions,

steamed pudding was well within everyone's reach.

Many considerations have removed the pudding from its prominent position, including lack of time and fear of excess animal-fat and carbohydrate intake. But it definitely deserves a place – even if one of diminished importance – in the diet. Steamed puddings are easy

to make and, crammed with fresh seasonal fruits and aromatic spices, take a lot of beating for sheer deliciousness. Once in a while they will not do any harm at all!

SUET LAYER PUDDING

This delicious pudding can be very heavy, so to lighten the load slightly I have replaced half of the flour with the same weight of fresh breadcrumbs.

Use any other fresh seasonal fruit for the layers, such as plums, damsons, gooseberries, rhubarb, raspberries and cherries. Serve with ice cream or custard.

▶ Grease a 1.15-litre/2-pint pudding basin with butter.

Place the flour, breadcrumbs and salt in a bowl. Rub in the suet until the mixture resembles fine breadcrumbs. Stir in enough water with a knife to give a soft but not too sticky dough.

Divide the dough into four pieces. Roll each piece of suet pastry into a circle separately, graduating to fit the size of the basin. Place the small circle in the basin.

Slice one-third of the apples over the pastry, and sprinkle with one-third of the lemon and orange rinds, cinnamon, sugar and cloves. Continue to layer in exactly the same way until all the fruit and pastry have been used.

Cover the basin with pleated greased foil and tie down with string. Steam for 2½ hours. *Check the liquid level frequently and add more boiling water if necessary.*

To serve, remove the foil, loosen the edges with a knife and turn out on to a warmed serving dish.

100 g/4 oz self-raising flour, sifted
100 g/4 oz fresh white breadcrumbs
pinch of salt
100 g/4 oz shredded beef suet
water to mix
675 g/1½ lb cooking apples, peeled and cored
grated rind of 1 lemon
grated rind of 1 orange
1 teaspoon ground cinnamon
1½ tablespoons soft brown sugar
¼ teaspoon ground cloves

CHRISTMAS PUDDING

225 g/8 oz self-raising flour, sifted
large pinch of salt
1 teaspoon grated nutmeg
1 teaspoon ground mixed spice
½ teaspoon ground allspice
275 g/10 oz shredded beef suet
275 g/10 oz fresh white breadcrumbs
225 g/8 oz rich dark brown sugar
450 g/1 lb raisins, stoned
450 g/1 lb sultanas
350 g/12 oz currants
100 g/4 oz candied peel
2 tablespoons finely chopped
    walnuts
1 small carrot, grated
1 apple, peeled and grated
6 eggs, beaten
grated rind and juice of 2 oranges
150 ml/¼ pint brown ale, stout or
    Guinness

This truly traditional English recipe was originally made with meat and first presented to William the Conqueror. Since then it has gone through many changes, and names, from 'Stewed Broth' to 'Christmas Pudding'. The fruit began to be added by the Elizabethans and gradually the meat was phased out completely and replaced by prunes, sultanas and plums.

Mature this Christmas pudding for at least 1 month before serving. Store in a ventilated dry place and steam again to reheat.

This recipe should make two 1.15-litre/2-pint puddings, or four 600-ml/1-pint puddings. My only word of warning is: do not let the puddings go off the boil at any time during cooking time as the overall timing will be wrong.

▶ Grease the pudding basins; have a large pan of boiling water ready.

Place all the dry ingredients in a bowl and mix thoroughly. Stir in the grated carrot and apple. Mix the eggs, orange rind and juice, and the ale in a bowl. Add to the dry mixture and stir well.

Turn into the prepared basins. Cover with pleated pieces of greased foil or greaseproof paper and tie down well with string. Place the basins in the fish kettle or saucepan with boiling water. Cover and steam large puddings for 6 hours and small ones for 4 hours. *Check the liquid level frequently and add more boiling water if necessary.* When cooked leave the foil on until they are cold. Replace the foil or paper with fresh pieces, and store in a dry cupboard until needed.

Steam again for a further 2 hours to reheat, and then turn out on to a hot dish. Serve with brandy butter.

TREACLE SPONGE

4 tablespoons golden syrup
1½ tablespoons fine white
   breadcrumbs
grated rind of 1 orange
100 g/4 oz butter, softened
100 g/4 oz caster sugar
2 large eggs, beaten
100 g/4 oz self-raising flour
½ teaspoon ground cinnamon
2 teaspoons Cointreau (optional)
milk to mix

My mouth starts watering at the slightest mention of this pudding. My mother makes the best treacle sponge in the world so I will treat you to a very similar version of her secret recipe. If you feel like having jam sponge instead, then replace the treacle with exactly the same quantity of jam, and follow the remainder of the recipe as below.

▶ Grease a 600-ml/1-pint pudding basin with butter.

Mix together the syrup, breadcrumbs and half of the orange rind in the basin. In a separate mixing bowl, beat the butter and sugar together until light and fluffy. Add the eggs gradually, beating well between each addition. Gently fold in the remaining orange rind, the flour and cinnamon. Stir in the liqueur and enough milk to make the mixture just loose enough to fall from a spoon. Add the mixture to the pudding basin.

Cover with a pleated piece of greased foil or greaseproof paper and tie down with string. Steam for 2½ hours. *Check the liquid level frequently and add more boiling water if necessary.*

To serve, remove the foil, loosen the edges with a knife and turn out on to a warmed serving dish.

JAM ROLY POLY

350 g/12 oz self-raising flour, sifted
pinch of salt
175 g/6 oz shredded beef suet
cold water to mix
8 tablespoons jam, for example,
   raspberry, strawberry, plum,
   cherry

The mention of roly poly brings a warm feeling to my heart. My school made the best version. I have tried several recipes to achieve that memorable perfection and this is definitely the closest I can get. Jam Roly Poly has to be served with custard for true tradition and a real school experience!

▶ Place the flour and salt in a bowl. Rub in the suet and add just enough water to mix with a knife to a soft dough.

Roll the pastry out on a floured board to a 25-cm/10-in × 35-cm/14-in rectangle. Spread the jam to within 2.5 cm/1 in of the edges. Dampen the edges and roll up, then pinch the edges to seal completely. Place in a double pleated piece of foil or greaseproof paper to allow for expansion during cooking. Seal completely.

Place in a steamer or covered saucepan half-filled with boiling water and steam for 2½ hours. *Check the liquid level frequently and add more boiling water if necessary.*

When cooked, remove the paper, slice and serve piping hot with custard.

BREAD AND BUTTER PUDDING

There are numerous recipes for bread and butter pudding. The original was plain as below, but people have since tarted it up with citrus peel, mixed fresh and dried fruit, liqueurs and even spices.

Experiment with it as you wish.

65 g/2½ oz butter, softened
4 thin slices of bread, crust removed
3 tablespoons currants
2 eggs
2 egg yolks, beaten
300 ml/½ pint milk
4 teaspoons caster sugar
¼ teaspoon grated nutmeg

▶ Grease four ramekins with a little of the butter. Spread the bread with the remaining butter and cut into strips. Arrange the bread in layers sprinkling each with currants. Finish with a layer of bread.

Mix together the eggs and egg yolks, milk, sugar and nutmeg in a jug and pour equal quantities over the four ramekins. Leave the bread to soak for 1 hour. Cover with pleated greased foil or greaseproof paper and tie down.

Steam over boiling water for 45 minutes. *Check the liquid level frequently and add more boiling water if necessary.*

Turn out on to individual plates to serve. This recipe is good both hot or cold. Serve with cream or yogurt.

STEAMED BATTER PUDDING

In the old days, these puddings used to be served plain with jam or marmalade sauce. I have laced them with currants, and then serve them with warmed honey.

175 g/6 oz plain flour, sifted
pinch of salt
2 eggs
grated rind of 2 oranges
300 ml/½ pint milk
50 g/2 oz currants or sultanas
5 tablespoons clear honey, warmed

▶ Grease 6–8 dariole moulds or ramekins with butter.

Place the flour, salt, eggs, orange rind and milk in a liquidiser or food processor.

Blend until smooth and bubbly. Spoon the currants and 1 teaspoon of the honey into the base of each dariole mould or ramekin. Pour on the batter. Cover with pleated greased foil or greaseproof paper and tie down.

Steam over boiling water for 20–25 minutes. Turn out on to serving dishes and spoon the remaining honey over the top. Serve hot.

FROM AROUND THE WORLD

The best recipes from traditional cuisine around the world are included in this chapter. If you love to experience the flavour and textures of all kinds of different foods, then these recipes will help to bring the exotic within your reach. Experiment with oriental specialities such as dim sum, sea bass with fermented black beans and fresh root ginger, and curries fragrant with spices; with colourful Mediterranean dishes, or a Caribbean chicken dish with delicious sweet potato, pumpkin and plantain among its ingredients. Choose your menu carefully, never having more than one rich course per meal, and remember that steaming will retain the maximum nutrients and taste in the food. If you wish to omit cream from a recipe, then just substitute fromage frais, quark or yogurt for a result that will be just as creamy but with a fraction of the calories.

Mixed Meat Dim Sum Balls (opposite)

SPICY MEAT DIM SUM BALLS

The Cantonese word 'dim sum' means 'eating snacks for pleasure' or 'order what you fancy'. They are served between the mid morning and late afternoon, and are now a favourite light and inexpensive lunch served with tea. In most restaurants, there are no menus but the waiters circle the tables with trollies laden with dozens of different dim sum, and it is up to you to choose what you want. Large groups can choose up to three or four dozen different little dishes, so you can imagine how much fun it can be.

Dim sum can be hot, sweet, sour, or spicy, and lots of them are cooked in the familiar bamboo steamers.

An easy selection of popular steamed dim sum follows.

225 g/8 oz glutinous rice, washed and soaked for 2 hours
225 g/8 oz minced pork
5 water chestnuts, chopped
1½ tablespoons soy sauce
salt and freshly ground black pepper
1 teaspoon curry powder

▶ Wash the soaked rice again and drain thoroughly. Place the pork and chestnuts in the food processor and mince until fine. Stir in the soy sauce, salt, black pepper and curry powder.

Using your hands, shape the mixture into small balls and roll them in the glutinous rice, cover thoroughly. Arrange on a wet piece of greaseproof paper in the steamer. Leave a small gap between each ball to allow for swelling during cooking. Cover with a tight fitting lid and steam over boiling water for 30 minutes. Serve hot or cold.

MIXED MEAT DIM SUM BALLS

Choose any variety of dried mushroom — even the Japanese ones are good. These little balls are steamed in a light noodle pastry skin; the recipe below shows you how to make the skins but they can be bought from most Chinese delicatessens; the bought variety keep well in the refrigerator for 10 days.

225 g/8 oz plain flour
1 large egg
1–2 teaspoons water
450 g/1 lb pork
350 g/12 oz peeled prawns (uncooked if possible)
4 dried Chinese mushrooms, soaked for 25 minutes and rinsed
1 onion, finely chopped
2 tablespoons soy sauce
1 teaspoon sesame oil
salt and freshly ground black pepper

▶ Place the flour and egg in a liquidiser or food processor. Blend with enough water to mix to a pliable dough. Roll out on flour or cornflour until the dough is paper thin. Cut into 7.5-cm/3-in squares.

Mince the pork, three-quarters of the prawns, the mushrooms, onion, soy sauce and oil and season well with salt and pepper.

Place 1 tablespoon of the meat mixture in the centre of the noodle skin, fold up the sides and squeeze together. Top each parcel with a prawn. Place in a tiered steamer. Cook the dim sum balls in batches if you haven't got a tiered steamer. Cover with a tight fitting lid and steam over boiling water for 25 minutes.

Serve hot or cold with extra soy sauce. MAKES 30

HOT CHICKEN BUNS

450 g/1 lb self-raising flour
100 g/4 oz sugar
250 ml/8 fl oz warm milk or water
25 g/1 oz lard
8 dried Chinese mushrooms, soaked
    in water for 25 minutes, rinsed
    and sliced
225 g/8 oz cooked boneless chicken,
    finely sliced
1 tablespoon oyster sauce
1 tablespoon hoisin sauce
small pinch of Chinese five-spice
    powder
1 small onion, finely chopped
2 chillies, deseeded and finely
    chopped
salt and freshly ground black pepper
1 tablespoon sesame or vegetable
    oil
150 ml/¼ pint chicken stock
2 teaspoons cornflour
12 squares of greaseproof paper

The Chinese have several varieties of flour which would be difficult for us to get. I use self-raising flour for this recipe as the texture of the finished bun is closest to the authentic Chinese one. Although the mixture is sweetened with sugar, it makes a light fluffy case for both sweet and savoury fillings. Steamed beef buns are a favourite in Hong Kong. Hoisin and oyster sauce are both available from good supermarkets, Chinese supermarkets and delicatessens. Hoisin sauce is made of soya beans, dried prunes and garlic, while oyster sauce – a great favourite in Chinese cooking – contains soy sauce and brine in addition to oysters. Chinese five-spice powder consists of ground star anise, anise pepper, fennel, cloves and cinnamon. Oriental stores and delicatessens stock it.

▶ Mix together the flour, sugar, milk or water, and lard, to a smooth dough. Cover with a damp towel and leave to rest in a warm place for at least 1 hour. Mix the mushroom, chicken, oyster sauce, hoisin sauce, five-spice powder, onion and chilli in a bowl. Season well with salt and black pepper.

Heat the wok or a deep frying pan. Add the oil. When hot, fry the chicken mixture for about 3 minutes. Blend the stock with the cornflour and pour over the chicken. Stir until the mixture thickens. Allow the mixture to cool.

The dough should have risen slightly. Knead on a lightly floured board. Roll into a 45.5-cm/18-in × 5-cm/2-in sausage. Cut into 12 equal pieces. Roll each piece into a 13-cm/5-in circle.

Place 1 generous spoon of mixture on the centre of each circle of dough. Gather up the edges, twist and squeeze to seal the top. Place each bun on a piece of greaseproof paper and arrange in the steamer. Cover with a tight fitting lid and steam over boiling water for 15 minutes. Splash with cold water to glaze and serve immediately.

VEGETABLE STEAMED DUMPLINGS

225 g/8 oz self-raising flour, sifted
salt and freshly ground black pepper
cold water to mix
100 g/4 oz carrots, finely chopped
4 spring onions, trimmed and finely
    chopped
2 celery sticks, finely chopped
15 g/½ oz fresh root ginger, peeled
    and grated
1 clove garlic, crushed
100 g/4 oz canned bamboo shoots,
    drained and finely chopped

These dumplings are delicious just steamed, but as an alternative serving suggestion, you could deep fry the steamed dumplings until golden brown, add salt, and serve immediately.

▶ Place the flour and a pinch of salt in a bowl. Pour in enough cold water to mix to a firm dough. Roll the dough into a long sausage about 5 cm/2 in. in diameter. Slice into 12 equal pieces and roll each piece into a 7.5-cm/3-in circle. Mix the carrot, spring onion, celery, ginger, garlic and bamboo shoots in a bowl. Season well with salt and black pepper.

Place 1 tablespoon in the centre of each round. Fold up the sides and squeeze to seal completely. Place the dumplings in the steamer. Cover with a tight fitting lid and steam over boiling water for 25 minutes. Drain. Serve hot or cold.

CHINESE STEAMED PANCAKES

Although steaming doesn't come into the recipe until the reheating process; it is a vital part of the overall cooking. If the pancakes were reheated in the oven they would dry out, while steaming gives the pancakes the authentic texture. Make large batches as they freeze beautifully, however make sure that you allow them to defrost properly before using. These pancakes are the traditional accompaniment to Peking Duck and are made with wheat instead of rice. Use them to accompany any other main meal dishes.

150 g/5 oz plain flour, warmed
pinch of salt
100 ml/4 fl oz boiling water
1 tablespoon sesame or groundnut
  oil

▶ Place the flour and salt in a bowl and gradually add the boiling water. Stir with a knife, and add more water if the mixture looks particularly dry. Knead on a floured board until smooth. Cover the dough with cling film and leave to rest at room temperature for 40 minutes.

Knead the dough again until it is smooth, dusting with flour if it is sticky. Roll the dough to a 23-cm/9-in-long sausage, 1.25 cm/$\frac{1}{2}$ in. in diameter. Cut the sausage into 10 equal pieces. Roll each piece into a tight ball.

Roll two balls at a time by dipping one side of one ball in the oil and placing oiled side on to the other ball to make two layers. Roll into a 15-cm/6-in circle.

Heat the oil in a wok or frying pan and fry the double pancake until it has cooked on the base. Flip over and cook the other side. Peel the pancakes apart and put to one side. Repeat with the remaining balls.

Before serving, steam the pancakes over boiling water for 7 minutes. Serve in a bamboo steamer if you have one, if not then on a warm plate.

FOOD FACTS

▶ Some of the ingredients used in the Chinese recipes in this chapter may be unfamiliar, so a brief summary follows, especially to explain their use and to supplement the headnotes to individual recipes and the Glossary of Ingredients starting on page 121.

Bamboo shoots These are readily available canned in water or brine. They are the creamy-coloured shoots of the bamboo plant and can be stored in fresh water in a covered container in the refrigerator for 1–2 weeks, as long as the water is changed daily.

Dried Chinese mushrooms Available from oriental supermarkets, these large mushrooms must be soaked in water before use. Their flavour is distinctive and the texture substantial, almost 'meaty'.

Glutinous rice Short-grain opaque white rice which develops a sticky consistency when cooked. Oriental shops stock it.

Groundnut oil Made from groundnuts, this bland oil is also known as peanut oil and arachis oil. The Chinese use it a lot in their cooking, sometimes flavouring it by frying garlic or a few slices of fresh root ginger in it.

Rice wine This clear white wine is more closely related to spirit or fortified wine than to ordinary white wine as we know it. It is used to enhance pork and chicken flavours and to add fragrance to all sorts of dishes. Sherry is a good substitute if you do not live anywhere near a good oriental supermarket.

Sesame oil Popular in Chinese cooking, the intensity of flavour varies according to the darkness and density of the oil, which depend on the degree of refinement it has undergone. Avoid the very dark variety. Health food stores,

supermarkets, delicatessens and oriental stores stock it.

Soy sauce Made from fermented soya beans, this is an essential condiment in Chinese cookery, used as extensively as salt is in the west. Most commonly it is dark and pungently flavoured, but a more delicate – yet very salty – light soy sauce is also available from supermarkets, delicatessens and oriental stores.

Water chestnuts A crunchy texture characterises these round white chestnuts. They are stocked in cans by supermarkets as well as by specialist shops.

CHINESE STEAMED RIBS

1 kg/2 lb pork spare ribs, separated
 and chopped into individual
 5-cm/2-in lengths
salt and freshly ground black pepper
150 ml/$\frac{1}{4}$ pint pork or chicken stock
2 tablespoons soy sauce
15 g/$\frac{1}{2}$ oz fresh root ginger, peeled
 and grated
25 g/1 oz fermented black beans,
 rinsed and coarsely chopped
2 cloves garlic, crushed
2 tablespoons sherry or rice wine
15 g/$\frac{1}{2}$ oz sugar
spring onion tassels to garnish
 (optional)

This is one of the most popular dim sum snacks. The ribs are so moist that they melt in your mouth.

▶ Season the ribs with salt and freshly ground black pepper.

Place in a saucepan with the stock and soy sauce. Bring to the boil and simmer for 10 minutes. Meanwhile mix together the remaining ingredients. Season well with salt and pepper. Drain the spare ribs and dry on absorbent kitchen paper. Spread each with the black bean mixture.

Arrange the ribs in the steamer, cover with a tight fitting lid and steam over boiling water for 1 hour. *Check the liquid level frequently and add more boiling water if necessary.*

Remove all surface fat before serving.

CHINESE STEAMED SEA BASS

The Cantonese love to steam any whole fish. The favourite is the sea bass which is of course expensive, so other whole fish such as snapper or bream will do perfectly well. Do rinse the fermented black beans as they can be very salty.

▶ Wash the cleaned fish under cold running water. Remove any remaining blood from behind the backbone, as it is bitter. Score the outside of the fish with a knife and rub in the salt, then place in a suitable dish.

Rinse the black beans thoroughly and chop them coarsely. Place them in a bowl with the spring onion, ginger, garlic, soy sauce and sugar. Heat the oil in a wok or frying pan until the oil is smoking. Remove the pan from the heat and pour the oil on to the black bean mixture. Let the sauce sizzle for a while, mix well and pour over the fish. Place the fish in a steamer, cover with a tight fitting lid and steam over boiling water for 20 minutes. (Follow the notes on **Improvising** on page 9 when steaming large fish such as this.)

Transfer to a serving plate, spoon over all of the sauce and garnish with spring onion tassels.

1.25 kg/2½ lb sea bass, cleaned
1 teaspoon salt
2 tablespoons fermented black beans, soaked for 30 minutes
bunch of spring onions, trimmed and finely chopped
1 tablespoon fresh root ginger, peeled and grated
5 cloves garlic, crushed
1 tablespoon light soy sauce
1 teaspoon sugar
3 tablespoons sesame or ground nut oil
Garnish
spring onion tassels
lemon twists (optional)

SOUTH ASIAN CURRY

15 g/½ oz butter
1 tablespoon mild curry powder
¼ teaspoon turmeric
¼ teaspoon Mexican chilli powder
¼ teaspoon crushed coriander seeds
¼ teaspoon cumin
1 kg/2 lb monkfish or any other firm white fish, boned and thickly sliced
1 tablespoon olive oil
4 cloves garlic, crushed
2 chillies, deseeded and finely chopped
2 onions, finely chopped
1 (400-g/14-oz) can chopped tomatoes
1 teaspoon caster sugar
salt and freshly ground black pepper
coriander or parsley sprigs to garnish

If this was being authentically made you would use the South Indian curry leaves and tamarind leaves but as these are practically impossible to get unless you live in an Indian community, I will be using more widely known spices.
Monkfish is perfect for this dish as it is firm fleshed and absorbs the flavours. Make this curry one day in advance to allow all the flavours to infuse.

▶ Heat the butter in a pan and fry the curry powder, turmeric, Mexican chilli powder, coriander and cumin for 3 minutes without burning. Stir in the fish and coat with the spices. Leave to one side for up to 2 hours (if you have time).

Heat the oil in a pan and fry the garlic, chilli and onion until cooked but not brown. Stir in the tomatoes and sugar. Season well with salt and pepper. Stir in the fish and spices. Pour the mixture into a suitable bowl. Cover with a piece of foil or greaseproof paper and tie down with string. Place in a steamer or covered saucepan half-filled with boiling water and steam for 15 minutes. Taste and adjust seasoning if necessary.

Serve on a bed of rice, garnished with coriander or parsley sprigs.

GIEMA CURRY

1 onion
15 g/½ oz fresh root ginger
2 cloves garlic
½ green pepper
½ red pepper
1 chilli
1 tablespoon olive oil
450 g/1 lb lean lamb or beef, minced
salt and freshly ground black pepper
1 (400-g/14-oz) can tomatoes
50 g/2 oz creamed coconut
1 cinnamon stick
3 cardamom pods
1 clove
1 allspice berry
2 teaspoons paprika
pinch of ground fennel
pinch of cumin seeds
pinch of ground coriander
1 large potato
225 g/8 oz podded fresh or frozen peas
coriander leaves to garnish

A traditional dish from Malaysia. This is a rich-tasting curry made from ground spices and mince, cooked in a delicate creamed coconut sauce. Make at least a day in advance to allow the flavours to permeate the meat.

▶ Roughly chop the onion, peel and grate the ginger, crush the garlic cloves. Deseed and chop the peppers, deseed and finely chop the chilli. Heat the oil in a heavy-based pan. Fry the onion, ginger, garlic, peppers, chilli and meat to brown slightly. Season with salt and pepper and remove from the heat.

Heat the tomatoes, with the coconut until boiling. Stir in the spices, then pour over the meat. Peel and cube the potato and add to the meat with the peas. Mix thoroughly to incorporate all of the ingredients. Transfer to a suitable dish.

Cover with a piece of foil and tie down with string. Place in a steamer or covered saucepan half-filled with boiling water and steam for 1½ hours to 1 hour 45 minutes. *Check the liquid level frequently and add more boiling water if necessary.*

Serve from the bowl or on a bed or rice, garnished with coriander leaves.

LAMB BIRIANI

The 'Birianis' are traditionally part of the grand festival dishes. Fine grained basmati rice was very much the rice to use, however it is now quite expensive. Use the American long grain rice for everyday use, but try to get the real thing if you can for festivals and parties. Make in advance and re-steam before serving.

▶ Take the lamb off the bone and cut into bite-sized pieces. Reserve the bones. Heat the butter in a pan. Fry the lamb to brown on all sides. Remove from the pan and put to one side. Fry the cardamoms, cloves and cinnamon stick in the same pan for 2 minutes, being careful not to burn them. Add the garlic, ginger and onion and continue to cook for 5 minutes. Stir in half the quantity of nuts and all of the sultanas. Return the meat to the pan. Season very well with salt and black pepper.

Lay a piece of wet greaseproof paper in the base of the steamer, and arrange the meat mixture on top. Wash the rice and put in a saucepan with the lamb bones and the water. Bring to the boil, cover the steamer and steam the meat over the rice for 12–15 minutes.

Mix the saffron or food colouring with the warm milk.

Remove the bones from the rice. Season very well with salt and black pepper. Place the rice on top of the meat, piling it up in the shape of a hill. Make a deep hole in the centre with the long handle of a wooden spoon. Dribble the saffron milk over the sides of the hill. Cover again and steam over boiling water for 1 hour. *Check the liquid level frequently and add more boiling water if necessary.*

To serve, transfer the rice mixture to a warmed serving dish, remove the cinnamon stick and mix gently. Garnish with sliced egg and tomatoes, and the remaining cashew nuts and almonds.

1.25 kg/2½ lb shoulder of lamb, trimmed
50 g/2 oz butter
4 whole cardamom pods
2 cloves
1 small cinnamon stick
2 cloves garlic, crushed
15 g/½ oz fresh root ginger, peeled and grated
1 large onion, roughly chopped
20 cashew nuts, toasted
20 almonds, toasted
1 tablespoon sultanas
salt and freshly ground black pepper
225 g/8 oz basmati rice
450 ml/¾ pint water
1 teaspoon saffron threads, or 2 drops yellow food colouring
2 tablespoons warm milk
Garnish
2 hard-boiled eggs, sliced
2 tomatoes, sliced

///// FOOD FACTS

▶ The essence of good cooking with spices often lies in the correct approach to their preparation. The processes of roasting, grinding and mixing the spices can be lengthy in totally authentic recipes.

A sturdy pestle and mortar provide the most satisfactory option for crushing tough seeds, particularly when the quantities are quite small.

Other unusual ingredients can often cause problems if you are not quite sure what to do with them. Creamed coconut, for example, comes in blocks which can be broken and dissolved in water or other liquid. It is also available in a canned, ready-dissolved form but take care to read the label as some brands are sweetened!

GREEK LAMB WITH YOGURT DRESSING

This recipe is both easy and delicious, but make sure you give yourself the time to marinate the meat as it is vital for the authentic Greek taste. Yogurt is common to a lot of Greek and Turkish dishes, as it seems to aid digestion.

1 kg/2 lb lamb, cut from the leg in
   bite-sized cubes
3 tablespoons dry sherry
2 cloves garlic, finely chopped
2 shallots, finely chopped
2 tablespoons olive oil
salt and freshly ground black pepper
1 green pepper, deseeded and cut
   into bite-sized pieces
8 cherry tomatoes
2 courgettes, thickly sliced
4 small onions, cut in halves or
   quarters (depending on size)
3 teaspoons chopped fresh mint
4 teaspoons chopped chives
150 ml/$\frac{1}{4}$ pint lamb or beef stock
150 ml/$\frac{1}{4}$ pint natural yogurt

▶ Trim any fat from the lamb and place in a shallow dish. Mix together the sherry, garlic, and shallot and half of the oil in a bowl. Season well with salt and pepper and spoon over the lamb. Cover with cling film and leave to stand for 12–24 hours.

Carefully remove the lamb from the marinade and dry on absorbent kitchen paper reserving the marinade for the dressing. Heat the remaining oil in a heavy-based pan. Fry the lamb cubes over high heat until brown on all sides. Stir in the pepper, tomatoes, courgette and onion, and season well with salt and pepper.

Cut a piece of foil large enough to seal the food completely. Spoon on the food, and sprinkle with half of the mint and chives. Pour the stock into the frying pan, and bring to the boil scraping the sediment from the base of the pan. Boil to reduce until syrupy. Pour over the meat. Fold up the edges and squeeze to seal the food.

Place in the steamer, cover with a tight fitting lid and steam over boiling water for 25–30 minutes. *Check the liquid level frequently and add more boiling water if necessary.*

Meanwhile bring the marinade to the boil in a pan. Stir in the remaining herbs. Taste and adjust seasoning if necessary. Leave to cool. Stir in the yogurt.

Remove the foil, and transfer the contents to a warmed serving plate. Spoon the dressing over the meat or serve separately.

From the top: Giema Curry (page 84); Dolmades (page 88)

DOLMADES

12 vine, cabbage or spinach leaves
1 tablespoon olive oil
1 onion, finely chopped
4 tablespoons long-grain rice
salt and freshly ground black pepper
pinch of allspice
pinch of crushed rosemary
juice of 1 lemon
100 g/4 oz mushrooms, wiped and
 sliced
300 ml/½ pint chicken stock
100 g/4 oz lean minced lamb
2 tablespoons chopped parsley
25 g/1 oz pine nuts (kernels)
1 teaspoon chopped fresh mint
lemon wedges to garnish (optional)

Some say Dolmades were originated by the Greeks as a starter and others argue that it was a main course invented by the Turks. They can be served as either. As vine leaves are often difficult to get hold of, cabbage or spinach leaves have proved to be the perfect substitute. If using canned vine leaves, treat them with care as they are immensely fragile.

▶ Steam the leaves for 30 seconds over boiling water. Lay out flat and dry on absorbent kitchen paper. If using canned vine leaves, just unravel them carefully without breaking. Heat the oil and fry the onion and rice until lightly coloured. Season well with salt and pepper.

Stir in the allspice, rosemary, lemon juice, mushroom and just enough stock to bring the liquid 2.5 cm/1 in above the top of the rice. Cover with a tight fitting lid and cook gently for 12 minutes. Leave to cool. Stir in the lamb, parsley, nuts and mint. Season once more with salt and pepper. Spoon about 2 teaspoons of the mixture on to each leaf and wrap up tightly. Pack the dolmades in layers in the steamer. Cover and steam over the remaining stock for 1 hour. *Check the liquid level frequently and add more boiling stock or water if necessary.*

Arrange the dolmades on a warmed serving dish. Serve with a bowl of chilled yogurt.

MOUSSAKA

2 large aubergines, diced
salt and freshly ground black pepper
2 tablespoons olive oil
2 large onions, finely chopped
2 cloves garlic, crushed
675 g/1½ lb cooked lamb, minced
675 g/1½ lb tomatoes, peeled,
 deseeded and chopped
pinch of dried thyme
pinch of dried rosemary
20 g/¾ oz butter
20 g/¾ oz plain flour
½ teaspoon mustard powder
250 ml/8 fl oz milk (infused with
 onion, mace, parsley stalks and
 peppercorns)
1 egg, separated
4–6 tablespoons grated Parmesan
 cheese

Moussaka has changed nationalities several times. Originally an Arabic dish it was seized by invading Turks, and now the Greeks have snatched it and call it their national dish. Whichever country claims it, it must be well worth the taste! There are more receipes for moussaka than Arabs in Arabia, so feel free to invent your own. The recipe below is the closest I can find to any original.

▶ Place the aubergines in a colander and sprinkle with plenty of salt. Leave to one side for 30 minutes. Rinse under cold water to remove the salt and bitter juices. Dry on absorbent kitchen paper.

Heat the oil in a pan. Fry the aubergine, onion and garlic until cooked, but not brown. Stir in the lamb, tomato, thyme, rosemary, aubergine, and seasoning. Spoon into a suitable bowl.

Melt the butter in a clean pan. Stir in the flour and mustard, cook for 2 minutes. Add the milk and bring to the boil, stirring constantly until thickened. Remove from the heat, whisk in the egg yolk. Season well with salt and freshly ground black pepper. Whisk the egg white to a stiff peak and fold into the sauce with the Parmesan. Pour over the meat. Cover with foil and tie down with string. Place in a steamer or covered saucepan half-filled with boiling water and steam gently for 15–20 minutes.

Heat the grill. Remove the foil and place the bowl under the grill until the surface is golden brown all over and serve at once.

AROZ CON POLLO

This is Spain's traditional chicken dish. Like most Spanish recipes, it contains saffron, which is the dried stamens of cultivated crocus.

Saffron contains a yellow colouring substance, giving many Spanish dishes that memorable yellow tinge. It is however very expensive to buy in England, so a cheaper alternative would be to add a couple of drops of yellow food colouring in place of the saffron. The guests need never know!

▶ Season the chicken breasts with lemon juice, salt and pepper. Heat the oil in a heavy-based pan and fry the chicken until golden brown on all sides. Transfer to a pudding basin. Fry the onion, garlic, pepper and rice in the same pan until the rice has turned white. Stir in the remaining ingredients. Season well with salt and pepper and pour over the chicken breasts. Cover with foil or greaseproof paper and tie down with string. Place in a steamer or covered saucepan half-filled with boiling water and steam for 40 minutes. *Check the liquid level frequently and add more boiling water if necessary.*

Remove the foil and spoon the cooked chicken and rice on to a warmed serving plate. Garnish with olives and flat-leaf parsley. Serve at once.

4 boneless chicken breasts
juice of $\frac{1}{2}$ lemon
salt and freshly ground black pepper
1 tablespoon olive oil
1 onion, finely chopped
2 cloves garlic, crushed
2 red peppers, deseeded and diced
300 g/10 oz long grain rice, well washed
1 (400-g/14-oz) can of chopped tomatoes
generous pinch of saffron
2 tablespoons chopped parsley
10 black olives, stoned and halved
1 teaspoon capers
300 ml/$\frac{1}{2}$ pint chicken stock
100 g/4 oz frozen peas, defrosted
Garnish
8 black olives, stoned
sprigs of flat-leaf parsley

STEAMED PAELLA

Anyone who has been to Spain will recognise this dish! It is a colourful assortment of meats, vegetables, spices and seafood, which is traditionally cooked and served in a special two-handled frying pan. You may vary the quantities of all the ingredients, except rice-to-stock ratio, at will.

▶ Heat the oil in a heavy-based pan, fry the chicken pieces to brown on all sides. Remove from the pan and put to one side. Fry the salami, onion, garlic, pepper and rice in the saucepan for 5 minutes to colour slightly and allow the rice to turn white.

Pour in enough stock to bring the liquid level 2.5 cm/1 in above the top of the rice. Return the chicken to the pan and stir in the fish and pimientos. Season well with salt and pepper. Cover with a tight fitting lid and steam for 15 minutes. Throw in all of the remaining ingredients and continue to steam for 5 minutes.

Pile the paella on to a warmed serving dish and garnish with lemon or lime wedges, olives and plenty of freshly chopped parsley.

2 tablespoons olive oil
3 boneless chicken or rabbit pieces, cut into bite-sized cubes
100 g/4 oz small spicy salami sausage, cut into cubes
1 onion, sliced
1 clove garlic, crushed
1 green pepper, deseeded and cut into strips
175 g/6 oz long-grain rice, well washed
chicken or fish stock
225 g/8 oz firm white fish, skinned and cubed
2 canned red pimientos, cut into strips
salt and freshly ground black pepper
12 prawns with shells, washed
12 mussels, scrubbed and beard removed
75 g/3 oz frozen or cooked fresh peas
Garnish
wedges of lemon or lime
black olives
chopped parsley

OSSO BUCO

1.5 kg/3½ lb shin of veal, cut into 3.5-cm/1½-in slices
salt and freshly ground black pepper
2 tablespoons olive oil
2 onions, finely chopped
2 cloves garlic, crushed
450 g/1 lb carrots, cut into thick matchsticks
4 celery sticks, roughly chopped
pinch of chopped fresh rosemary
pinch of chopped fresh thyme
300 ml/½ pint veal or chicken stock
300 ml/½ pint dry white wine
1 (400-g/14-oz) can tomatoes
1 teaspoon sugar
Garnish
2 tablespoons chopped parsley
grated rind of 1 lemon
2 cloves garlic, finely chopped

This is a fabulous inexpensive Italian stew using the cheaper shin bone of veal. The name Osso Buco means hollow bone. When buying, check whether the butcher will cut the shin into slices, as it will reduce the preparation time dramatically. I have suggested the traditional Italian garnish for extra authenticity.

▶ Season the meat with salt and pepper. Heat the oil in a heavy-based pan and fry the veal pieces until golden brown on all sides. Remove from the pan and put to one side. Fry the onion, garlic, carrot and celery for 3 minutes to brown slightly. Season well with salt and pepper.

Place a piece of wet greaseproof paper in the steamer. Arrange the vegetables on top. Stand each piece of meat upright on top of the vegetables to prevent the bone marrow from escaping during cooking. Sprinkle the meat with rosemary and thyme.

Place the stock, wine, tomatoes and sugar in a saucepan. Bring to the boil. Place the steamer full of veal and vegetables on top. Cover with a tight fitting lid and steam for 2 hours. *Check the liquid level frequently and add more boiling stock if necessary.*

Transfer the meat and vegetables to a warmed serving dish. Boil the tomato mixture to reduce to a rich sauce consistency. Taste and adjust seasoning if necessary. Pour over the meat and sprinkle with parsley, lemon rind and garlic.

RATATOUILLE

1 large aubergine, cubed
6 courgettes, thickly sliced
salt and freshly ground black pepper
2 tablespoons olive oil
2 large onions, sliced
3 cloves garlic, crushed
2 green peppers, deseeded and diced
450 g/1 lb tomatoes, peeled, deseeded and quartered
2 tablespoons chopped parsley
¼ teaspoon chopped fresh or dried oregano
¼ teaspoon chopped fresh or dried marjoram
1 tablespoon chopped fresh basil
chopped fresh basil or parsley to garnish

Ratatouille is a wonderfully rich vegetable stew that benefits from very slow cooking.

Make sure you use olive oil to keep that authentic taste of provincial France. Serve on its own with crusty brown bread, or as a vegetable accompaniment for meat and poultry.

▶ Place the aubergine and courgette in a colander. Sprinkle with plenty of salt and leave for 30 minutes. Rinse thoroughly under the cold water tap to remove the salt and dry on absorbent kitchen paper.

Heat the oil in a pan and fry the onion, garlic and pepper until cooked, but not brown. Stir in the aubergine, courgette, tomato and herbs. Season well with salt and black pepper and fry for 3 minutes.

Pour into a pudding basin, cover with foil or greaseproof paper and tie down with string. Place in a steamer or covered saucepan half-filled with boiling water and steam for 1 hour. *Check the liquid level frequently and add more boiling water if necessary.*

Remove the foil and serve piping hot, garnished with chopped basil or parsley.

Ratatouille is also delicious served cold as a salad.

HUNGARIAN FISH

1.25 kg/2½lb firm white fish fillets,
   skinned
salt and freshly ground black pepper
juice of ½ lemon
25 g/1oz butter
2 onions, sliced
1 clove garlic
6 tomatoes, peeled, deseeded and
   sliced
1 tablespoon chopped fresh herbs,
   for example, dill, parsley, fennel
2 teaspoons paprika
150 ml/¼ pint soured cream
Garnish
paprika
sprigs of fresh herbs

Any firm white fish may be used for this recipe, however the Hungarians always use freshwater fish (such as carp), as Hungary is a country without a coastline. The most important ingredient is paprika; that subtle Hungarian spice with the distinctive red colour. This dish should be served on a bed of buttered noodles, and if you pop the fresh noodles into the boiling water during the last five minutes of the steaming time, then all the food will be ready together with no more washing up to do.

▶ Season the fish with salt, black pepper and lemon juice. Cut into bite-sized pieces and lay in a suitable bowl. Heat the butter and fry the onion and garlic until cooked but not brown. Stir in the tomato and herbs and season well with salt and pepper. Spoon over the fish. Mix the paprika with the soured cream and gently stir into the fish and vegetables. Cover the bowl with foil or greaseproof paper and tie down with string. Place in a steamer or covered saucepan half-filled with boiling water and steam for 20 minutes.

   Transfer to a warmed serving dish. Sprinkle with paprika and sprigs of fresh herbs.

GEFILTE FISH

1 slice of fresh white bread
water to soak
1 tablespoon oil
1 large onion, finely chopped
1 carrot, grated
1 kg/2 lb mixed white fish fillets
2 tablespoons chopped parsley
salt and freshly ground black pepper
2 eggs
capers
300 ml/½ pint strong fish stock
Garnish
flat-leaf parsley
lemon wedges

A section of traditional dishes from around the world would not be complete without the famous Jewish Gefilte Fish. In the old days, the women would finely chop the fish and stuff it into the skin of a carp and poach in jellied fish stock. Nowadays, everyone just minces the fish to make glorious tasting fish balls. So this is an interesting and unusual first or main course that can be made in advance.

The more varieties of fish used, the better the end result, but you may use just one kind of fish for an everyday version.

▶ Soak the bread in the water for 15 minutes. Meanwhile heat the oil in a saucepan and fry the onion and carrot for 3 minutes. Mince together the fish, onion, carrot and parsley. Season well with salt and pepper.

   Squeeze the water out of the bread, and add the bread and eggs to the fish mixture. Mix well to incorporate all ingredients thoroughly. Use your hands to form the mixture into balls the size of plums. Top each one with a caper.

   Place in a steamer, cover with a tight fitting lid and steam over the fish stock for 30 minutes. *Check the liquid level frequently and add more boiling stock if necessary.*

   Transfer the balls to the serving plate. Boil the stock to reduce until syrupy. Taste and adjust seasoning if necessary. Pour over the fish balls. Cool and place in the refrigerator to chill before serving. Garnish with sprigs of flat-leaf parsley and lemon wedges.

STEAMED CHICKEN CARIBBEAN

Sweet potatoes, pumpkin and plantains all conjure up the true meaning of Caribbean cooking.

If you live in or near a West Indian community, you will see these and other exotic fruits and spices on sale.

Supermarkets are now selling sweet potato and pumpkin, so have a go at this recipe for a taste of the Caribbean.

▶ Season the chicken with salt, pepper and lemon juice. Heat the oil in a heavy-based pan. Fry the chicken over high heat to brown on all sides. Remove and put to one side. Fry the onion, garlic, ginger, chilli and tomato until cooked but not brown. Stir in the sweet potato, pumpkin and plantain. Season well with salt and black pepper.

Spoon the vegetables and spices into a steamer. Sit the chicken on top. Bring the stock to the boil and stir in the cinnamon stick. Cover the chicken mixture with a tight fitting lid and steam over the boiling stock for 1½ hours. *Check the liquid level frequently and add more boiling stock if necessary.*

Remove the cinnamon stick. Transfer the chicken to a hot serving plate and keep warm. Blend the vegetables and the stock in a liquidiser or food processor. Spoon over the chicken. Garnish with slices of lemon and parsley sprigs.

Serve at once.

1 (1.75-kg/4-lb) oven-ready chicken, giblets removed
salt and freshly ground black pepper
juice of 1 lemon
1 tablespoon oil
1 onion, finely sliced
3 cloves garlic
15 g/½ oz fresh root ginger, peeled and grated
2 chillies, deseeded and finely chopped
3 tomatoes, peeled, deseeded and chopped
675 g/1½ lb sweet potato, peeled and cubed
675 g/1½ lb pumpkin, peeled and cubed
2 plantains, roughly sliced
600 ml/1 pint chicken stock
1 cinnamon stick
Garnish
lemon slices
flat-leaf parsley sprigs

BABOTIE

It is convenient to find that the famous South African dish, babotie, is the perfect rechauffé dish. It was introduced in the 17th century by Muslim slaves who made it from leftover meat and vegetables. Fish can be used instead, so empty the refrigerator on Monday after a large Sunday lunch and follow the outlines of the recipe below using whatever ingredients you want.

▶ Soak the bread in the milk. Grease a pudding basin with a little butter. Gently fry the onion, garlic, celery and carrot in the butter until cooked but not brown. Stir in the curry powder, chutney, lemon juice and fish or meat. Season well with salt and black pepper. Spoon into the pudding basin. Squeeze the milk from the bread, reserving the milk, and fork the bread into the meat mixture.

Mix the eggs with the reserved milk. Season well with salt and black pepper. Pour the topping over the meat. Arrange the blanched almond halves over the top. Cover with a piece of foil or greaseproof paper and tie down. Place in a steamer or covered saucepan half-filled with simmering water and steam gently for 40 minutes or until the custard is set.

Serve sprinkled with chopped parsley.

1 slice of white bread
300 ml/½ pint milk
1 onion, finely chopped
2 cloves garlic, crushed
2 celery sticks, roughly chopped
4 cooked carrots, sliced
25 g/1 oz butter
3 teaspoons curry powder
1 tablespoon mango chutney
juice of 1 lemon
675 g/1½ lb cooked meat or fish, for example, lamb, beef, chicken, white fish, minced
salt and freshly ground black pepper
Topping
2 eggs
12 blanched almonds, toasted
chopped parsley to garnish

PASTA, PULSES & GRAINS

Pasta, pulses, rice and other grains can supply the starchy part of a main course in place of potatoes, dumplings or pastry. The basis of pasta is durum wheat which grows particularly well in Italy. It is ground into semolina, and mixed to a smooth paste with oil and water, then spinach purée or egg are sometimes added. Moulded into various shapes and sizes pasta is often dried before being sold. The most common pulses are yellow and green peas, haricot, butter and red kidney beans and yellow, green and red lentils. Most need to soak in water for several hours before cooking, unlike vegetables. There are many varieties of rice, the grain which forms the staple diet of a large proportion of the world's population: white polished, brown unpolished, wild, long-grain or patna rice, and the best quality Basmati rice. Round-grain rice is suitable for risottos and puddings where the grain needs to be very absorbent. Follow the recipe for steamed rice and you will not end up with a starchy mess.

Couscous (page 109)

RAVIOLI NAPOLETANA

Once you know how to make the pasta cushions, you may let your imagination run riot and fill them with whatever you fancy.

I will be filling mine with a classic mixture of spinach and curd cheese and steaming the whole dish in a rich Italian tomato sauce.

Home-made ravioli will never be exactly like the bought variety, but it is an exciting and delicious treat to serve up at any meal.

▶ Place the flour, semolina and salt in a bowl. Make a well in the centre and put in the oil, eggs and half of the water or milk. Mix well, gradually incorporating the dry ingredients. Add more liquid when necessary. Work the paste into a smooth and firm dough. Knead well, cover with a cloth, and leave to rest for 30 minutes.

Meanwhile make the filling. Place the spinach in a pan over high heat to evaporate all of the water. Dry on absorbent kitchen paper. Place in a bowl with the ricotta. Mix well and season with salt, pepper and nutmeg. Leave to one side.

Dust the work surface with flour, cut the ravioli dough in half and roll each half until paper thin. Brush one thin sheet of pastry with water and place a generous teaspoon of filling at regular intervals on the pastry. Place the other sheet of pastry on top of the fillings with floured hands; press the top piece down around each mound of filling. Stamp each one out with a fluted cutter or cut squares with a pastry wheel. Leave the shapes to dry for 2 hours. Place in a large pan of boiling salted water and cook for 5 minutes. Rinse under cold water.

To make the sauce, melt the butter in a pan and fry the onion and garlic until cooked but not brown. Stir in the remaining ingredients and season well with salt and pepper.

Place the ravioli and tomato sauce in a pudding basin. Cover with foil or cling film (it will not melt) and place in a steamer. Cover with a tight fitting lid and steam over boiling water for 15 minutes.

Pile on to a warmed serving dish and garnish with sprigs of fresh basil. Serve immediately. MAKES 16

Ravioli paste
225 g/8 oz plain flour, sifted
50 g/2 oz semolina
pinch of salt
1½ tablespoons olive oil
2 eggs, beaten
3–4 tablespoons water or milk
Filling
225 g/8 oz chopped frozen spinach
50 g/2 oz ricotta or cream cheese
salt and freshly ground black pepper
pinch of grated nutmeg
Napoletana sauce
15 g/½ oz butter
1 large onion, sliced
1 clove garlic, crushed
50 ml/2 fl oz red wine
1 (400-g/14-oz) can chopped
  tomatoes
1 tablespoon tomato purée
1 bay leaf
¼ teaspoon sugar
150 ml/¼ pint meat or vegetable
  stock
2 teaspoons chopped fresh basil
sprigs of basil to garnish

CANNELLONI

25 g/1 oz butter
25 g/1 oz plain flour
150 ml/$\frac{1}{4}$ pint milk
salt and freshly ground black pepper
2 tablespoons chopped parsley
pinch of oregano
pinch of marjoram
1 egg yolk
1 tablespoon oil
225 g/8 oz boneless chicken, finely chopped
75 g/3 oz cooked ham, finely diced
1 onion, finely chopped
2 cloves garlic, crushed
1 green pepper, deseeded and finely chopped
1 celery stick, finely chopped
12–16 cannelloni (allow 3–4 per person)
1 (400-g/14-oz) can chopped tomatoes
1 teaspoon sugar
150 ml/$\frac{1}{4}$ pint chicken stock
25 g/1 oz Parmesan cheese, grated

This is a classic Italian pasta dish. Pasta literally means a paste of flour and water. Dried cannelloni tubes can be bought from delicatessens and supermarkets nowadays.

If you follow the guidelines of my recipe below you may substitute any meat and vegetable with ingredients of your choice. This dish can be assembled in advance and steamed just before serving.

▶ Melt the butter in a pan, stir in the flour and cook for 2 minutes. Add the milk and bring to the boil, stirring constantly. Season with salt and pepper, stir in the herbs and simmer for 3 minutes. Remove from the heat and stir in the egg yolk. Cover and keep to one side.

Heat the oil in a pan and fry the chicken, ham, onion, garlic, green pepper and celery for 6 minutes, stirring occasionally. Season well with salt and pepper. Leave to cool, then stir in the herb sauce.

Place the cannelloni in a large pan of boiling salted water and cook for 5 minutes. Lift out and dip them into a bowl of ice-cold water. Dry on absorbent kitchen paper. Place the filling in a forcing bag with a large plain nozzle (or use the handle of a spoon). Pipe (or spoon) into the cannelloni tubes and then place them in a suitable bowl.

Mix the tomatoes, sugar and stock together and pour over the cannelloni. Cover with foil or greaseproof paper and tie down with string. Place in a steamer or covered saucepan half-filled with boiling water and steam for 40 minutes. *Check liquid level frequently and add more boiling water if necessary.*

Just before serving heat the grill. Remove the foil or paper and sprinkle the surface with Parmesan. Grill until the top is golden brown and serve immediately.

ANGEL HAIR PASTA

450 g/1 lb strong white flour, warmed in the oven
2 large eggs
1$\frac{1}{2}$ tablespoons olive oil
100 ml/4 fl oz water

Pasta, like bread and potatoes, used to be branded as a starchy food which caused obesity. Thankfully for all pasta lovers, it is now considered wholesome and healthy! Fresh pasta is now readily available in most supermarkets. If you want to make your own pasta, then follow this simple recipe.

▶ Place all the ingredients in a food processor and process for 1 minute. Cover the dough with cling film and leave to sit for 1 hour at room temperature. Divide the dough into 10 equal pieces. Flour a work surface and roll the dough until paper thin; you should be able to see right through the dough.

Dust the sheets with flour and lay on a wire rack to dry for 1 hour. To cut into angel hair, spread out the sheets of pasta and cut into very thin strips. Coil up about 20 at a time, very loosely, and put to one side. Cover with cling film until needed.

TAGLIATELLE WITH GAMMON AND MUSHROOMS

The beauty of this dish is that the topping steams over the cooking tagliatelle and everything is ready at the same time. Perfect for the cook who can never get everything ready at the same time! This makes an ideal lunch or light supper dish. If using fresh tagliatelle then cook three minutes before serving, otherwise follow my receipe.

▶ Drain the gammon and dry on absorbent kitchen paper. Heat the oil in a pan and gently fry the onion and garlic until cooked but not brown. Stir in the gammon and mushroom. Continue to fry for 3 minutes. Mix in the tomatoes, herbs and tomato purée. Season well with salt and pepper. Pour into a pudding basin. Cover with foil or cling film (it will not melt). Bring a large pan of salted water to the boil. Place the pudding basin in a steamer and cover with a tight fitting lid. Steam over the water for 25 minutes. *Check the liquid level frequently and add more boiling water if necessary.*

Fifteen minutes before serving, place the tagliatelle in the boiling water, cover and continue to steam the food above for 12 minutes.

Drain the pasta and pile on to a warmed serving dish, dot with butter and season with salt and pepper. Remove the foil from the bowl and spoon the gammon and sauce over the pasta. Sprinkle with Parmesan, garnish with basil, if liked and serve immediately.

350 g/12 oz lean gammon, cubed and soaked for 15 minutes
1 tablespoon olive oil
1 onion, finely sliced
1 clove garlic, crushed
175 g/6 oz mushrooms, wiped and sliced
1 (400-g/14-oz) can chopped tomatoes
1 tablespoon chopped fresh basil
1 tablespoon chopped parsley
1 tablespoon tomato purée
salt and freshly ground black pepper
225 g/8 oz dried tagliatelle
15 g/$\frac{1}{2}$ oz butter
50 g/2 oz Parmesan cheese, grated
sprigs of basil to garnish (optional)

NORTH COUNTRY LAMB

A warming meal of lamb with succulent haricot beans and fresh root vegetables. This recipe is best made in advance and reheated.

▶ Drain the haricot beans and boil in clean water for 20 minutes. Drain well. Heat the oil in a heavy-based pan and fry the lamb until brown on all sides. Transfer to a large pudding basin. Fry the vegetables in the same pan for 5 minutes and spoon over the lamb. Stir in the drained beans. Season very well with salt and freshly ground black pepper.

Pour the stock into the frying pan, stir in the rosemary, mint and redcurrant jelly. Bring to the boil, scraping the sediment from the base of the pan. Pour over the lamb. Cover with foil and tie down with string. Cook in a steamer or covered saucepan half-filled with boiling water for 1$\frac{1}{2}$ hours. *Check the liquid level frequently and add more boiling water if necessary.*

Arrange the meat and vegetables on a warmed serving dish and keep warm. Boil any remaining stock until rich and syrupy, tasting and adjusting seasoning as necessary.

Pour over the meat and garnish with sprigs of rosemary and mint.

225 g/8 oz dried haricot beans, soaked overnight
2 tablespoons oil
1 (1-kg/2-lb) boned leg of lamb
1 large onion, sliced
1 small swede, peeled and cubed
1 large turnip, peeled and cubed
2 cloves garlic, crushed
1 parsnip, peeled and cubed
salt and freshly ground black pepper
150 ml/$\frac{1}{4}$ pint lamb or beef stock
$\frac{1}{2}$ teaspoon fresh or $\frac{1}{4}$ teaspoon dried rosemary
1 teaspoon chopped mint
1 tablespoon redcurrant jelly
sprigs of rosemary and mint to garnish

WEST COUNTRY HAM ROLLS

People have combined ham and peas for hundreds of years, and as the mix tastes so good, I am sure we will continue to do so into the future.

This makes a wonderful high protein lunch dish to serve with plenty of crusty bread and butter, or is just as good for a late night supper in front of the box.

Assemble the rolls in advance and steam them just before serving. Get hold of some 'no soak' peas if you can. If not, soak the same quantity of ordinary dried peas in cold water overnight and boil until soft.

► Place the peas in a pan and follow the packet instructions. Boil until they are soft. Mash with a fork to a smooth paste. Leave to get cold and firm. Place the milk in a pan with the onion, bay leaf, and peppercorns. Bring to the boil, remove from the heat and leave to infuse for 15 minutes.

Heat the oil in a pan and fry the spring onion and garlic until cooked but not brown. Remove from the heat. Stir in the mashed peas, half of the cress, the wholegrain mustard and beaten egg. Season well with salt and black pepper. Divide the mixture between the slices of ham and roll up. Lay side by side in a gratin dish.

Melt the butter in a pan and stir in the flour, mustard powder and seasonings. Cook for 2 minutes. Strain the milk on to the butter mixture and bring to the boil, stirring constantly. Simmer for 3 minutes and pour the sauce over the ham rolls. Cover with foil or greaseproof paper and place in a steamer or place on top of a saucepan. Cover with a tight fitting lid and steam over boiling water for 15 minutes.

Heat the grill. Remove the foil or greaseproof paper and sprinkle the rolls with Cheddar. Grill until the surface is golden brown. Sprinkle with the remaining cress and serve at once.

100 g/4 oz 'no soak' dried peas
300 ml/½ pint milk
1 slice of onion
1 bay leaf
6 black peppercorns
1 tablespoon oil
4 spring onions, trimmed and finely chopped
1 clove garlic, crushed
punnet of mustard cress
¼ tablespoon wholegrain mustard
1 egg, beaten
salt and freshly ground black pepper
8 (5-mm/¼-in) slices lean cooked ham
20 g/¾ oz butter
20 g/¾ oz plain flour
pinch of mustard powder
salt and cayenne
50 g/2 oz Cheddar cheese, grated

Opposite From the top:
West Country Ham Rolls; Tagliatelle with Gammon and Mushrooms (page 97)

FOOD FACTS

► Pulses are a rich source of protein and are regaining status as a frequent ingredient in the diet. This is due to the increased interest in vegetarian food and the concern for including ample fibre in the diet.

The popularity of pulses has never waned in the middle east, central America, or India, where chick peas, red kidney beans and lentils, respectively, have always played leading roles in native dishes.

Soaking overnight in cold water is a necessary preliminary step to cooking most pulses; the purpose is to re-hydrate the food and thereby ensure a sensible cooking time. A speedier way of achieving this is to cover the pulses with water in a saucepan and bring slowly to a rapid boil, then cover, turn off the heat and leave for 2 hours before cooking. Red lentils are one of the exceptions: they do not require pre-soaking and

they become tender within about 15 minutes cooking time. The other pre-eminently important point to remember is to bring dried red kidney beans to the boil, then boil rapidly for 3 minutes at the start of the cooking time, in order to destroy poisonous enzymes that are naturally present. Remember that canned beans are an excellent and time-saving alternative.

BUTTER BEAN RAMEKINS

100 g/4 oz dried butter beans,
  soaked in cold water overnight
25 g/1 oz butter
225 g/8 oz leeks, trimmed, washed
  and finely chopped
2 cloves garlic, crushed
bunch of watercress, rinsed and
  roughly chopped
3 egg whites
salt and freshly ground black pepper
generous pinch of mace
150 ml/¼ pint double cream
watercress sprigs to garnish

This recipe is ideal as a vegetarian meal with crusty brown bread and salad or as a tasty vegetable accompaniment for meat and poultry. It can be made in advance and served hot or cold. For a first course, serve with watercress sauce.

▶ Grease four ramekins with a little butter or oil.

Drain the butter beans and place in a large pan with fresh water. Bring to the boil and cook for 40 minutes. Drain and dry on absorbent kitchen paper.

Melt the butter in a pan and fry the leek and garlic until cooked but not brown. Place the beans, leek mixture and watercress in a food processor and blend until smooth. Add the egg white and continue to blend until absolutely smooth. Season with salt, pepper and mace. With the machine running, pour in the cream. Do not process for more than 20 seconds.

Spoon the mixture into the prepared ramekins. Cover each with foil or cling film and place in a steamer. Cover with a tight fitting lid and steam over boiling water for 35 minutes.

Turn the mousse out on to four serving plates and garnish with watercress sprigs.

RED BEANS AND RICE LOUISIANA

225 g/8 oz dried red kidney beans,
  soaked in water for 8 hours
25 g/1 oz butter
1 onion, finely chopped
4 celery sticks, finely chopped
3 cloves garlic, crushed
100 g/4 oz long-grain rice, well
  washed
ham or chicken stock
2 tablespoons chopped parsley
1 bay leaf
10 drops Tabasco sauce
salt and freshly ground black pepper
450 g/1 lb smoked sausage or salami,
  cut into bite-sized cubes
chopped parsley to garnish

Food is a favourite subject in New Orleans. Apparently people spend so much time debating the pros and cons of different foods that I suspect they talk of little else.

This recipe is a favourite during the famous Mardi Gras jazz festival. Large bowls of it are consumed with salad and crusty bread.

▶ Drain the kidney beans and place in a saucepan. Add enough fresh water to cover the beans and bring to the boil. Boil for 3 minutes, reduce the heat, then cover and cook for 45 minutes. Drain and rinse.

Meanwhile melt the butter in a pan and gently fry the onion, celery, garlic and rice until the rice turns white and the onion is cooked. Add enough stock to bring the level of liquid about 2.5 cm/1 in above the top of the rice. Add the beans and stir in the parsley, bay leaf and Tabasco. Season the mixture well with salt and pepper.

Cover with a tight fitting lid and steam for 30 minutes. Throw in the cubes of sausage and continue to steam for 5 minutes.

Remove the bay leaf and pile the mixture on to a warmed serving dish; sprinkle with parsley and serve at once.

EXOTIC SHELLFISH TIMBALE

This is an unusual and exceptionally tasty mixture of seafood and vegetables steamed to perfection in a thin suet crust.

Use my recipe as a guideline and add any mixture of seafood and vegetables. Make sure you check the seasoning well as shellfish can sometimes be quite bland.

▶ Place the flour in a bowl and rub in the suet and salt until the mixture resembles breadcrumbs. Mix with enough water to make a smooth pliable dough. Roll out and line a 1.15-litre/2-pint pudding basin, retaining one-third of the pastry for the lid. In lining the basin and sealing the pastry lid, follow the instruction given for Steak and Kidney Pudding on page 66.

Melt the butter in a pan, and fry the spring onion and peppers for 5 minutes. Stir in the rice, sweetcorn, peas, herbs, chutney and curry powder. Gently fold in the shellfish. Season the mixture well with salt and pepper and pile into the suet-lined basin. Roll out the remaining pastry, dampen the edges and stick down to make the lid. Cover the basin with foil and tie down with string. Place in a steamer or covered saucepan half-filled with boiling water and steam for 1 hour. *Check the liquid level frequently and add more boiling water if necessary.*

To serve, remove the foil and loosen the edges with a knife. Turn out on to a warmed serving plate. Garnish the top with sprigs of dill and parsley.

225 g/8 oz self-raising flour
100 g/4 oz shredded beef suet
pinch of salt
water to mix
25 g/1 oz butter
4 spring onions, trimmed and finely chopped
1 green pepper, deseeded and diced
1 red pepper, deseeded and diced
50 g/2 oz brown rice, cooked
100 g/4 oz sweetcorn kernels, fresh or frozen
100 g/4 oz peas, fresh or frozen
3 tablespoons chopped parsley
1 teaspoon chopped fresh dill
2 tablespoons mango chutney
1 tablespoon mild curry powder
100 g/4 oz peeled, cooked prawns
75 g/3 oz mussels, shelled
1 (200-g/7-oz) can white crab meat
salt and freshly ground black pepper
sprigs of dill and parsley to garnish

PILAU RICE

Colourful pilau rice is India's traditional accompaniment to curry and tandoori dishes. It is usually made with the fine Basmati rice which has a distinctive authentic flavour. However, as it is expensive, it is perfectly all right to use the cheaper long-grain rice instead.

▶ Drain the rice and rinse thoroughly, leave to drain, shaking occasionally. Deseed and finely chop the pepper and chilli. Heat the oil in a frying pan. Fry the onion, garlic, pepper and chilli until cooked but not brown. Stir in the rice and spices. Fry until the rice turns white. Season well with salt and black pepper. Pour on enough stock to bring the liquid 2.5 cm/1 in above the top of the rice. Cover with a tight fitting lid and steam for 15–20 minutes.

Fluff up the rice mixture with a fork. Taste and adjust seasoning if necessary. Serve hot, garnished with coriander leaves.

225 g/8 oz Basmati or long-grain rice, soaked for 20 minutes
1 green pepper
1 red chilli
1 tablespoon vegetable oil
1 small onion, finely chopped
2 cloves garlic, crushed
½ teaspoon ground cumin
¼ teaspoon turmeric
¼ teaspoon ground coriander
salt and freshly ground black pepper
chicken stock or boiling water
coriander leaves to garnish

SPICY RICE MUSHROOMS

This dish is immensely versatile. Serve it as a light lunch with salad or as a substantial first course for dinner. I would also serve it as a vegetable accompaniment to poultry and fish dishes. The recipe below contains no meat, so it is ideal for vegetarians, but feel free to add cooked chicken or seafood for an interesting alternative.

1 tablespoon oil
4 large flat mushrooms, wiped and
   stalks finely chopped
2 shallots, finely chopped
1 clove garlic, crushed
1 chilli, deseeded and finely chopped
7 g/$\frac{1}{4}$ oz fresh root ginger, peeled
   and grated
1 teaspoon hot curry powder
$\frac{1}{4}$ teaspoon ground cumin
50 g/2 oz long-grain rice, well
washed
tomato juice
salt and freshly ground black pepper
chopped parsley to garnish

▶ Heat the oil in a pan and fry the chopped mushroom stalks, shallot, garlic, chilli, ginger, spices and rice until the shallot is cooked and the rice has turned white.

Pour on enough tomato juice to bring the liquid level 2.5 cm/1 in above the top of the rice. Season well with salt and pepper, cover with a tight fitting lid and cook for 15 minutes.

Pile the rice on to the mushrooms and place in the steamer. Cover with a tight fitting lid and steam over boiling water for 5 minutes.

Sprinkle with parsley and serve at once. Follow our colourful serving suggestion, if liked.

PRAWN AND HAM JAMBALAYA

Ever since my husband went to New Orleans during the Mardi Gras festival he has encouraged me to dabble with some of the wonderful Cajun and Creole dishes that he tried. We so enjoyed them that I now want him to take me there and see it all for real!

▶ Deseed and roughly chop the peppers. Melt the butter in a large pan and fry the peppers, celery, onion, garlic and rice, until the onion is cooked and the rice has turned white. Stir in the parsley, tomatoes and Tabasco. Season very well with salt and pepper.

Add enough water to bring the liquid level about 2.5 cm/1 in above the top of the rice. Cover with a tight fitting lid and steam for 15 minutes. Throw in the prawns, ham and peas. Cover and continue to cook for 5 minutes.

Pile on to a warmed serving plate, garnish with lemon twists and parsley sprigs and serve at once.

1 green pepper · 1 red pepper
50 g/2 oz butter
4 celery sticks, sliced
1 large onion, finely sliced
2 cloves garlic, crushed
100 g/4 oz long-grain rice
3 tablespoons chopped parsley
1 (400-g/14-oz) can chopped
  tomatoes
6 drops Tabasco sauce
salt and freshly ground black pepper
450 g/1 lb peeled, cooked prawns
450 g/1 lb cooked ham, roughly
  chopped
100 g/4 oz peas, fresh or frozen
Garnish
lemon twists
flat-leaf parsley sprigs (optional)

CHINESE STEAMED RICE WITH CHICKEN

4 chicken breasts
salt and freshly ground black pepper
2 tablespoons soy sauce
1 tablespoon sherry or rice wine
2 teaspoons oyster sauce
15 g/½ oz fresh root ginger, peeled
 and grated
2 cloves garlic, crushed
225 g/8 oz long-grain rice, well
 washed
100 g/4 oz canned sliced bamboo
 shoots
2 celery sticks, roughly chopped
½ small cabbage, shredded
spring onion tassels to garnish

The Chinese are experts where rice is concerned. They eat huge quantities in either fried or steamed form everyday with every meal.

Here are the golden rules to steaming perfect rice. Firstly wash the rice in several changes of water until the water becomes clear. The second rule is to cover the rice with no more or less than 2.5 cm/1 in of water. This avoids sticky glutinous over-cooked rice.

The last important rule is never to peek into the rice pot during the cooking time as the valuable steam will escape, and that will send your cooking time up the spout. Do not use easy-cook rice for this recipe as it lacks the starchy taste and texture which is so important to Chinese rice. This dish is a favourite amongst Cantonese people.

▶ Season the breasts with salt and pepper. Mix together the soy sauce, sherry or rice wine, oyster sauce, ginger and garlic and pour over the chicken. Leave to marinate for up to 2 hours.

Place the rice into a large saucepan, and add enough water to bring the liquid level about 2.5 cm/1 in above the top of the rice. Bring to the boil. Add the chicken and marinade. Reduce the heat to as low as possible, cover with a tight fitting lid and steam for 20 minutes. During the last five minutes, throw in the prepared vegetables. Cover again and continue to steam for 5 minutes.

Pile the food on to a warmed serving dish and serve piping hot, garnished with spring onion tassels.

CLASSIC RISOTTO

50 g/2 oz butter
1 large onion, finely chopped
1 red pepper, deseeded and finely
 diced
2 cloves garlic, crushed
450 g/1 lb cooked chicken or beef,
 diced
225 g/8 oz long-grain rice, well
 washed
salt and freshly ground black pepper
pinch of saffron
rich chicken or beef stock
100 g/4 oz peas, fresh or frozen
50 g/2 oz Parmesan cheese, grated

Risotto is exceptionally easy to prepare and is the perfect dish for using up all sorts of meat and vegetables left over from previous days.

It is of course a classic Italian dish and there are quite literally millions of recipes. Follow mine as a rough guide and have some fun.

▶ Melt the butter in a large pan. Fry the onion, pepper and garlic until cooked but not brown. Stir in the chicken and rice and fry until rice turns white. Season very well with salt, pepper and saffron. Pour on enough stock to bring the liquid level about 2.5 cm/1 in above the top of the rice. Bring to the boil. Cover with a tight fitting lid and cook over the lowest heat for 15 minutes. Stir in the peas, cover and continue to cook for 5 minutes.

Stir in the Parmesan. Check seasoning, adjust if necessary and serve immediately.

BREAKFAST KEDGEREE

It is odd to think that what we know as a traditional English breakfast is in fact Indian in origin. Unfortunately, the old country house breakfasts are quite rare nowadays, their long sideboards laden with silver dishes of bacon, eggs, devilled kidneys, kippers and kedgeree.

Although I might call this recipe 'Breakfast Kedgeree', it does make a perfect light lunch dish and is also excellent for a late night supper in front of the box.

▶ Place the haddock in the milk and leave to soak for 30 minutes.

Melt the butter in a large pan and gently fry the onion and rice until the onion is cooked and the rice has turned white. Stir in the curry powder and parsley and season well with salt and black pepper. Add enough water to bring the liquid level about 2.5 cm/1 in above the top of the rice. Bring to the boil. Drain the haddock and discard the milk. Place the haddock in the steamer, cover and steam over the rice for 15–20 minutes. Flake into bite-sized pieces. Check that the rice is tender and gently fold in the haddock and chopped egg. Taste and adjust seasoning if necessary. Pile on to a warmed serving plate and sprinkle with plenty of chopped parsley.

450 g/1 lb smoked haddock, skinned and boned
150 ml/¼ pint milk
25 g/1 oz butter
1 large onion, finely chopped
225 g/8 oz long-grain rice, well washed
2 teaspoons curry powder
2 tablespoons chopped parsley
salt and freshly ground black pepper
4 hard-boiled eggs, finely chopped
chopped parsley to garnish

BOKARI PILAF

A delicious rich meal-in-one dish that is quick to prepare and best eaten as soon as it is ready.

You may use Patna, Basmati, or American long-grain rice. This dish is perfect for cleaning the larder of old vegetables, so you can use whatever you have and follow the basic method through.

▶ Season the chicken livers with salt and pepper. Heat the oil in a pan and fry the onion and leek until cooked but not brown. Stir in the rice, and fry until the rice turns white.

Mix the turmeric, tomatoes and parsley and add to the rice mixture. Pour on enough boiling stock to bring the liquid level 2.5 cm/1 in above the top of the rice. Cover the pan with a tight fitting lid and steam for 15 minutes. Add the mushroom, peas and seasoned livers, cover and continue to cook for 5–8 minutes. Season with salt and pepper to taste.

Transfer the rice mixture to a heated serving dish and garnish with tomato slices and sprigs of parsley. Serve at once.

450 g/1 lb chicken livers, washed and sinew removed
salt and freshly ground black pepper
1 tablespoon olive oil
1 large onion, sliced
1 small leek, trimmed, washed and finely chopped
225 g/8 oz white rice
½ teaspoon turmeric
1 (200-g/7-oz) can tomatoes
2 tablespoons chopped parsley
300 ml/½ pint chicken stock
100 g/4 oz mushrooms, wiped and sliced
100 g/4 oz frozen peas
Garnish
sliced tomatoes
flat-leaf parsley sprigs

SAVOURY CORN BREAD

1 tablespoon olive oil
1 small onion, finely chopped
175 g/6 oz plain flour, sifted
175 g/6 oz cornmeal, polenta or
  maize meal
2 teaspoons baking powder
salt and freshly ground black pepper
2 eggs, beaten
1 tablespoon clear honey
300 ml/½ pint milk
50 g/2 oz Gruyère cheese, grated
2 tablespoons chopped chives

One of the most popular cereals used in cooking is cornmeal, also known as maize meal or polenta. It is easily recognised by its vivid yellow colour and nutty flavour. You will find cornmeal in health food shops, delicatessens and some supermarkets.

The Americans first introduced us to corn bread as a nourishing and delicious accompaniment to a meal or just on its own, served warm with lashings of butter. To make a sweet bread, omit the cheese and add dried fruit and sugar.

▶ Grease and line a 450-g/1-lb loaf tin. Heat the oil in a pan and fry the onion until cooked but not brown. Place the flour, cornmeal, baking powder, salt and pepper in a large bowl.

In another bowl mix together the eggs, honey, milk, cheese and chives. Stir the egg mixture into the flour mixture and add the onions. Mix well to a smooth thick batter.

Spoon the mixture into the prepared loaf tin. Cover with pleated foil or greaseproof paper and tie down with string. Steam over boiling water for 1 hour. *Check the liquid level frequently and add more boiling water if necessary.*

Remove the foil and turn the bread out on to a wire rack to cool slightly. Serve warm with butter.

FOOD FACTS

▶ Happily influenced by a great variety of exotic cuisines, the repertoire of recipes using grain is extending, creating many new nutritious and gastronomic possibilities. Cornmeal, which is also known as maize-meal and polenta, is ground from yellow or white corn. Its potential has long been exploited in the United States, in dishes such as the famous cornbreads and pancakes, traditionally served for breakfast. A nutty flavour and bright yellow colour characterise cornmeal.

Another grain which is quite familiar to the health-food shopper is nutty-flavoured bulgar, also called cracked wheat or burghul. Its evolution begins with the wholewheat grain, which is cracked between rollers. Then it is hulled and parboiled, and features in famous dishes such as Tabbouleh salad from the Middle East. Discover its potential in Chick Pea and Bulgar Hot Pot on page 108.

From the top: Chick Pea and Bulgar Hot Pot (page 108); Ravioli Napoletana (page 95)

POLENTA PUDDING

25 g/1 oz butter or beef dripping
675 g/1½ lb lean beef mince
1 onion, finely chopped
1 carrot, finely chopped
2 celery sticks, finely chopped
150 ml/¼ pint beef stock
1 bay leaf
2 teaspoons Worcestershire sauce
2 tablespoons tomato ketchup
salt and freshly ground black pepper
Batter
1 tablespoon olive oil
1 onion, finely chopped
2 cloves garlic, crushed
75 g/3 oz plain flour
75 g/3 oz fine cornmeal
1½ teaspoons baking powder
pinch of salt
1 tablespoon sugar
1 egg · 150 ml/¼ pint milk
50 g/2 oz Cheddar cheese, grated
2 tablespoons chopped parsley

This is a tasty alternative version of Shepherd's Pie, the base being a savoury mince and the topping a light corn sponge. (Polenta is another name for cornmeal.) The mince can be made in advance and frozen, but the topping needs to be assembled just before serving.

Try this once and you might never go back to Shepherd's Pie. It has become a favourite supper dish in my home.

▶ Melt the butter or dripping in a frying pan and fry the mince to brown well. Add the onion, carrot and celery and continue to fry for 5 minutes. Stir in the beef stock, bay leaf, Worcestershire sauce and ketchup. Season very well with salt and freshly ground black pepper. Cover and simmer for 15 minutes.

Meanwhile make the batter. Heat the oil and fry the onion and garlic until cooked but not brown. Place the flour, cornmeal, baking powder, salt and sugar in a bowl. In a separate bowl, mix the egg, milk, Cheddar and parsley. Stir the egg mixture into the flour mixture and add the onion and garlic. Mix to a smooth batter. Pour the mince into the base of a 1.15-litre/2-pint pudding basin. Spoon on the batter. Cover with a pleated piece of foil or greaseproof paper and tie down with string.

Place in a steamer or covered saucepan half-filled with boiling water and steam for 35 minutes. Remove the foil or paper and serve straight from the bowl.

CHICK PEA AND BULGAR HOT POT

225 g/8 oz dried chick peas, soaked
   overnight
50 g/2 oz butter
1 large onion, sliced
2 cloves garlic, crushed
2 celery sticks, finely chopped
4 small carrots, thickly sliced
2 leeks, trimmed, washed and
   thickly sliced
4 turnips, peeled and quartered or
   cubed, according to size
100 g/4 oz bulgar wheat, washed
1 (400-g/14-oz) can chopped
   tomatoes
2 tablespoons chopped chives
pinch of thyme
salt and freshly ground black pepper
chopped chives to garnish

This dish is a nutritional paradise for vegetarians, brimming with vital proteins and minerals. I am not a vegetarian but I love food like this, and so I sometimes add pieces of boneless chicken or lamb. Bulgar is simply wheat that has been partially cooked and dried. You may recognise its other names: cracked wheat or burghul. It has a fabulous nutty taste and can always be used in place of rice, or can be soaked and then served in salads.

▶ Place the chick peas in a large pan of boiling water, boil briskly for 10 minutes then simmer for 1 hour.

Meanwhile melt the butter in a pan. Gently fry the onion, garlic, celery, carrot, leek and turnip for 5 minutes. Stir in the bulgar, tomatoes and herbs. Bring to the boil. Season well with salt and pepper. Pour into a pudding basin and place in a steamer. Cover with a tight fitting lid and steam over the simmering chick peas for 35–40 minutes. Check that the chick peas are tender, and stir them into the tomato mixture. Check seasoning and adjust if necessary.

Pile into a warmed serving bowl and garnish with chives.

COUSCOUS

I have to admit that this recipe was not written by me at all! How could I possibly attempt to better the sheer perfection of my mother's own recipe. She has kindly allowed me to share her secret with you.

Couscous is a classic North African dish made up of two parts; La marga, which is a pot-au-feu containing the meat and assorted vegetables, some essential and some optional; and the steamed couscous, which is a type of semolina. Couscous was originally made in a couscoussier but if you are like me and do not have one, then a large saucepan or stock pot with a steamer or colander will do the job perfectly well. Try to get hold of a fiery sauce called Harissa. It is the perfect accompaniment and can be bought in delicatessens.

3 tablespoons olive oil
1 kg/2 lb stewing lamb, cubed, fat removed
1 (1.5-kg/3-lb) roasting chicken, jointed into 8 pieces
1 large onion, roughly chopped
pinch of saffron (optional)
small stick of cinnamon
450 g/1 lb tomatoes, peeled, deseeded and chopped
450 g/1 lb carrots, quartered
100 g/4 oz chick peas, soaked overnight
2 chillies, deseeded and chopped
1 cabbage heart, washed and quartered
2 large turnips, peeled and thickly sliced (optional)
225 g/8 oz pumpkin, peeled and cubed (optional)
4 large courgettes, thickly sliced
2 tablespoons raisins
2 teaspoons chopped fresh coriander
1 teaspoon cayenne
salt and freshly ground black pepper
675 g/1½ lb couscous
melted butter
sprigs of coriander to garnish

▶ Heat the oil in a large pan and fry the lamb until golden brown on all sides. Transfer to a saucepan or base of a couscoussier. Fry the chicken in the same pan to brown on all sides and lay over the lamb. Fry the onion to brown and add to the chicken and lamb. Pour in just enough water to cover the food. Bring to the boil, skimming off all dirty foam and add more cold water to replace what has been skimmed off. When clear, stir in the saffron, cinnamon, tomato and carrot. Drain the chick peas and rinse thoroughly under cold running water. Add to the meat and vegetables. Cover the pan and simmer gently for 1½–2 hours. (If done in advance and cooled, any solidified fat can be removed). Add the chilli, cabbage, turnip, pumpkin, courgette, raisins, chopped coriander and cayenne. Season well with salt and pepper.

Place the couscous in a basin of cold water and leave for 15 minutes. Remove the bones from the meat and discard. Put the meat back in to the saucepan.

Line a steamer, colander or the top of a couscoussier with muslin. Drain the couscous and put it into the muslin. Bring the meat and vegetables to the boil. Put the top section in place and tie a tea-towel around the join to prevent steam escaping. Cover and leave to steam for 30 minutes.

Tip the couscous into a bowl of cold water and stir with a fork to separate any lumps. Drain well.

If you have bought Harissa sauce, stir 1 tablespoon of Harissa into about 300 ml/½ pint of stock. Reheat, stirring.

To serve, pile the couscous on to a warmed serving plate and pour the melted butter over it. Arrange the best pieces of meat and vegetables on top of the couscous. Garnish with sprigs of coriander. Pour the remaining meat, vegetables and chick peas into a warmed bowl and serve separately to moisten the couscous.

Put the fiery sauce on the table as it can then be used as a relish. SERVES 8

SWEET SUCCESS

If you want to avoid pastries and sugary, fatty puddings, then what is left to offer your family and guests? The best and simplest everyday answer is fresh seasonal fruit. Now that exotic imports, such as mango, passionfruit and starfruit, boost home-grown fruits during winter months, there is always a profusion of colourful and fragrant ingredients to select from. With this in mind, I have designed a number of recipes to allow for substitutions so that you may include the choicest fruits available to enhance dessert presentation. With a little imagination and hardly any trouble this chapter offers ideas that maximise the natural sweetness of fresh and dried fruit. However, there are a few stodgy favourites for those who may feel cheated! After all, who can resist the occasional richly delicious treat.

Steamed Pudding with Exotic Fruit Sauce (page 120)

STEAMED NECTARINES WITH MELON APRICOT SAUCE

I can think of nothing I'd like better than to finish every meal with this pudding. It is healthy, light and completely delicious. If fresh apricots are out of season, then you may use canned apricot halves in natural juice. I have suggested Charentais melon because of its beautiful orange flesh but any melon will do: if using honeydew melon, then cut the quantity by half as they are so much bigger.

▶ Pare the rind of half of the orange and lemon. Cut into needleshreds and blanch for 20 seconds. Keep to one side.

Bring the melon, apricots and juice of the orange and lemon to the boil. Simmer for 10 minutes. Stir in the ground almonds, almond essence and sugar. Blend in a liquidiser or food processor until smooth.

Place the nectarines in a bowl and pour the purée over them. Cover with a piece of foil and place in the steamer. Cover with a tight fitting lid and steam over boiling water for 15 minutes.

Remove the paper. Arrange the nectarines on warmed plates. Sieve the sauce and spoon it over the nectarines. Sprinkle with flaked almonds and needleshreds of orange and lemon. Serve hot or cold.

1 orange
1 lemon
½ Charentais melon, peeled, deseeded and roughly chopped
6 fresh apricots, peeled, stoned and roughly chopped
50 g/2 oz ground almonds
3 drops almond essence
1 tablespoon sugar
4 nectarines, halved and stoned
Garnish
25 g/1 oz toasted flaked almonds
needleshreds of orange and lemon

KIWI WITH GOOSEBERRY AND RASPBERRY PURÉE

This is another perfect recipe for those of you who have gardens overflowing with gooseberries and raspberries. These two fruits together make a colourful piquant purée that complements the delicate taste of the kiwi.

Feel free to use different fruits for the purée if you want, but make sure that they are at their peak of ripeness if fresh. Frozen or canned fruit work just as well.

▶ Place the gooseberries, raspberries, lemon rind and juice, sugar and orange juice in a pan. Bring to the boil, stirring, and gently simmer for 10 minutes.

Blend the mixture in a liquidiser or food processor and sieve to remove the pips. Stir in the liqueur. Cut four 25-cm/10-in-square pieces of foil. Divide the purée between the four pieces of foil. Top with slices of kiwi and a sprig of mint. Fold up the edges and seal completely. Steam over boiling water for 5 minutes.

Allow your guests to open their parcels at the table. Serve with fromage frais or natural yogurt.

225 g/8 oz gooseberries, topped and tailed
225 g/8 oz raspberries
grated rind and juice of ½ lemon
25 g/1 oz sugar
juice of 1 orange
2 tablespoons raspberry liqueur (or Kirsch)
8 kiwi fruit, peeled and sliced
4 small sprigs of mint

JAZZ BANANAS

2 oranges
225 g/8 oz strawberries, hulled
4 drops vanilla essence
2 tablespoons raspberry or
    strawberry liqueur
4 large bananas, halved lengthways
4 Victoria plums, stoned and
    roughly chopped
4 apricots, stoned and roughly
    chopped
sprigs of mint to garnish

A favourite of mine from my childhood. Make sure you choose fruit at their peak of ripeness. Of these, bananas are the only vital ingredient, and you can substitute any of the others to your own taste.

▶ Pare the rind from the oranges and cut into thick needleshreds. Blanch for 10 seconds and keep to one side. Cut away the peel and pith and carefully remove the orange segments. Discard the pips.

Place the orange, with any juice, and the strawberries in a liquidiser, and blend until smooth. Stir in the vanilla essence and liqueur.

Cut four 35-cm/14-in-square sheets of foil. Place 2–3 tablespoons of purée on each piece, arranging the banana, plums and apricots on top. Add a sprig of mint and some needleshreds to each. Fold up the edges of the foil to seal the parcels completely.

Steam over boiling water for 3 minutes. Let your guests have the pleasure of opening them. Serve with sweetened fromage frais or quark.

PEARS IN SPICED RED WINE

grated rind and juice of 2 lemons
300 ml/$\frac{1}{2}$ pint red wine
1 cinnamon stick
$\frac{1}{2}$ teaspoon ground mixed spice
2 drops vanilla essence
75 g/3 oz caster sugar
4 firm pears, cored and peeled, stalk
    left on
$\frac{1}{2}$ teaspoon arrowroot
2 strips angelica, soaked in water

For this recipe you may use either the tall slim conference pear or the large oval Comice, or even the medium-sized tapering Williams pear.

Whichever variety you prefer, try to buy pears that are the same size and shape, as this makes the presentation of the dish so much better. Pears bruise easily, therefore I suggest that you core them before peeling and use lemon juice to prevent the flesh turning brown. The dish can be made in advance as it is served cold.

▶ Place the rind and juice of the lemon in a pan with the wine, cinnamon stick, mixed spice, vanilla essence and caster sugar. Bring to the boil, stirring frequently until the sugar has dissolved.

Put the prepared pears in a bowl and pour the wine mixture all over. Cover with a piece of foil or greaseproof paper and tie down with string. Place in a steamer or covered saucepan half-filled with boiling water and steam for 30–40 minutes. *Check the liquid level frequently and add with more boiling water if necessary.*

Leave the pears to cool in the red wine. When cold remove the cinammon stick. Stand the pears in a serving dish. Boil the red wine mixture to reduce it to 150 ml/$\frac{1}{4}$ pint. Mix the arrowroot with a little of the juice. Pour back into the pan, bring to the boil and simmer for 2–3 minutes stirring constantly. Leave to cool. Drain the angelica and dry on absorbent kitchen paper. Cut into leaf shapes or diamonds. Press two pieces of angelica into each pear either side of the stalk. Strain the spiced wine sauce over the pears to glaze.

STEAMED FIGS WITH ORANGES

Try hard to get fresh figs, but if it proves impossible, then use dried ones soaked in orange juice for 1 hour.

▶ Pare the rind from three of the oranges and cut into julienne strips. Reserve. Squeeze the juice from these oranges. Cut away the peel and white pith of the remaining oranges and carefully remove the orange segments. Remove pips. Add any juice to the squeezed quantity. Strain it all through a sieve into a saucepan. Stir in one tablespoon of the Grenadine and the Cointreau. Place the orange rind strips in a saucepan with the remaining Grenadine and the water. Boil until almost all the liquid has evaporated and the strips have turned pink. Remove and dry on absorbent kitchen paper.

Lay a piece of wet greaseproof paper on the base of a steamer. Arrange the whole figs and orange segments on top. Cover with a tight fitting lid. Steam over the boiling orange juice for 3–5 minutes. Meanwhile put the caster sugar on a plate and use to coat the strips of orange peel. Keep the fruit warm whilst finishing the sauce.

Boil to reduce by half. Remove from the heat. Stir in the fromage frais or quark. Flood four plates with the sauce. Arrange the steamed fruit on top and garnish with sugared orange strips.

6 small blood oranges
3 tablespoons Grenadine syrup
1 tablespoon Cointreau
4 tablespoons water
12 whole fresh figs
1 tablespoon caster sugar
100 g/4 oz fromage frais or quark

CALVADOS APPLES WITH VANILLA CREAM

A pudding for all seasons that is deliberately flavoured with fruit liqueur: use cognac if preferred. Pears can be substituted for the apples.

▶ Bring the Calvados, orange juice, lemon juice, raspberry liqueur and honey to the boil, stirring well. Peel and core the apples. Set in a small bowl. Pour over the Calvados mixture. Cover the bowl in foil. Place in the steamer. Cover with a tight fitting lid and steam over boiling water for 15 minutes.

Meanwhile make the vanilla cream. Bring the milk, sugar and vanilla pod to the boil. Beat the egg yolks in a mixing bowl. Pour on the milk mixture, stirring steadily. Mix well and return to the pan. Stir over a gentle heat until the mixture thickens. *Do not boil.* Stir in the fromage frais or quark.

Remove the apples from the Calvados mixture and arrange them on a serving dish. Mix the arrowroot with 2 tablespoons of the mixture until smooth, pour the Calvados mixture into a pan, and stir in the arrowroot mixture. Bring to the boil, stirring carefully until the sauce thickens. Spoon over the apples, and garnish with a sprig of mint. Serve hot or cold with the vanilla cream.

50 ml/2 fl oz Calvados
juice of 1 orange
juice of 1 lemon
1 tablespoon raspberry liqueur
1 tablespoon clear honey
4 Granny Smith apples
Vanilla cream
300 ml/$\frac{1}{2}$ pint skimmed milk
2 tablespoons of sugar
1 vanilla pod or several drops vanilla
   essence
2 egg yolks
100 g/4 oz fromage frais or quark
$\frac{1}{4}$ teaspoon arrowroot
sprigs of mint to garnish

TIPSY FRUIT

450 ml/¾ pint Sauternes wine
12 large prunes
12 dried figs
8 dried apple rings
8 dried apricots
Apricot cheese
225 g/8 oz dried apricots
1 cinnamon stick
150 ml/¼ pint orange juice
100 g/4 oz fromage frais or quark
pared rind of ½ orange, cut into thin
   strips

Drunken fruit on a bed of creamy apricot cheese. If Sauternes is too difficult or expensive to get, you could use a medium sweet white wine and add a tablespoon of sugar. It is possible to get packets of mixed dried fruit rather than searching high and low for individual items.

▶ Boil the Sauternes to reduce by half. Place in a bowl with the fruit and cover with a piece of foil. Steam over boiling water for 15 minutes. *Check the liquid level frequently and add more boiling water if necessary.* Meanwhile make the cheese. Place the apricots, cinnamon stick and orange juice in cupped foil then seal the edges together carefully. Place in the steamer with the other fruit and steam for 10 minutes.

Remove the cinnamon stick. Blend the apricots and orange juice, with the fromage frais or quark, in a liquidiser or food processor until smooth. Blanch the thin strips of orange peel in the base of the steamer for 20 seconds. Cool in cold water.

Make a bed of apricot sauce on each of four plates. Remove the foil from the bowl of mixed fruit. Arrange the fruit and garnish with strips of orange.

ALL FRUIT CLAFOUTIS

Clafoutis was originally a rustic French pudding made with unstoned fruit. If you value your teeth I would suggest stoning fruit as the taste is exactly the same but the decision is yours. Any fruit will do but remember to keep small fruit whole if you decide not to stone them.

▶ Wash and dry the fruit. Place in a suitable bowl (that fits into the steamer). Sprinkle with the sugar.

Place all the batter ingredients in a bowl, except for the egg white. Mix to a smooth cream consistency. Whisk the egg white until stiff and gently fold into the batter mixture.

Spread over the fruit and sprinkle with the toasted almonds. Cover the bowl with foil or greaseproof paper and tie down. Place in a pan of boiling water or in a steamer, cover with a tightly fitting lid and steam for 45 minutes.

Remove the paper or foil and serve from the bowl with fresh cream or yogurt.

225 g/8 oz black cherries
225 g/8 oz apricots, quartered
225 g/8 oz black and red plums, quartered
2 nectarines, peeled and cut into bite-sized pieces
225 g/8 oz damsons
25 g/1 oz sugar
75 g/3 oz toasted almonds, roughly chopped

Batter
175 g/6 oz self-raising flour
25 g/1 oz ground almonds
1 teaspoon baking powder
25 g/1 oz caster sugar
4 drops almond essence
150 ml/$\frac{1}{4}$ pint milk
1 egg, separated

CHAMPAGNE SUMMER BERRIES WITH ALMOND BISCUITS

Biscuits
2 egg whites
50 g/2 oz caster sugar
75 g/3 oz ground almonds
16 sweet almond halves
Berries
225 g/8 oz strawberries, hulled and quartered
225 g/8 oz raspberries
100 g/4 oz redcurrants, topped and tailed
100 g/4 oz blackcurrants, topped and tailed
100 g/4 oz blackberries, hulled (optional)
25 g/1 oz caster sugar
juice of 1 lemon
250 ml/8 fl oz chilled Champagne

If you are lunching out-of-doors on a fabulous English summer's day, what better way to complement your main course than to serve the lightly steamed fruits of our land in sparkling champagne!

▶ Make the biscuits. Whisk the egg whites until stiff. Whisk in 2 teaspoons of the sugar until stiff and shiny. Fold in the remaining sugar and the ground almonds. Fill a piping bag with the mixture and pipe whirls the size of large walnuts on non-stick bakewell paper. Top each one with almond halves. Bake in a moderate oven (180 C, 350 F, gas 4) for 20 minutes until golden. Cool on a wire rack and keep fresh in an airtight tin.

Mix the berries together in a pudding basin. Sprinkle with half of the sugar and half of the lemon juice. Leave to sit for 10 minutes. Meanwhile pour the remaining sugar on to a large plate. Dip the rims of four glass dessert bowls into the remaining lemon juice, shake off the excess, then dip each dish into the sugar. Cover the pudding basin with foil and tie down. Place in a steamer or covered pan half-filled with boiling water and steam for 3–5 minutes.

To serve, spoon the fruit into the prepared dishes being careful not to ruin the frosted rim. At the table, pour the chilled champagne on to the fruit. Serve with the almond biscuits.

CRÈME BRÛLÉE

450 ml/¾ pint double cream
4 egg yolks
2 tablespoons caster sugar
4 drops vanilla essence
2–3 tablespoons demerara sugar

Crème Brûlée is rich baked custard where cream has been substituted for milk. Custards need delicate treatment, since if they are subjected to too much heat and overcooking, they will curdle and weep and be completely ruined. Therefore make sure you steam them gently and set the kitchen timer so as not to forget about them. Crème Brûlée should be made in the morning before serving, or even the night before if you prefer.

▶ Grease four ramekins with butter or oil. Heat the cream until just below boiling. Whilst the cream is heating, blend the egg yolks and sugar together in a mixing bowl. Pour on the cream and stir well. Strain the custard and stir in the vanilla essence. Place in the steamer and steam over simmering water for 10 minutes.

Chill in the refrigerator for at least 4 hours.

Heat the grill. Sprinkle the tops of the custards generously with demerara sugar to cover the surface. Place under the grill. Turn the ramekins round in order to brown and caramelise the sugar evenly. Chill in the refrigerator to harden the topping.

PEACH CARAMEL CUSTARD

A pretty orange custard surrounded by dark caramel. You can easily use canned peaches if fresh are out of season. It is vital that the custard does not get too hot during steaming, as the eggs will scramble.

▶ Place the granulated sugar in a heavy-based saucepan with the water. Melt the sugar gently over a low heat. When completely melted, boil until it turns a rich caramel brown colour. Pour into the base of a 1.15-litre/2-pint pudding basin. Bring the milk and almond essence to the boil. Meanwhile beat the cornflour, eggs, egg yolks, caster sugar and lemon rind to a smooth paste. Pour the milk gradually on to the egg mixture, stirring well.

Rinse the pan. Reserving half a peach for garnish, blend the peaches in a liquidiser or food processor and stir into the custard. Strain the mixture into the clean pan and heat, stirring well to a thick creamy consistency. *Do not boil.* Pour on to the caramel. Cover the bowl thoroughly with cling film (it will not melt), and place in a steamer. Cover with a tight fitting lid and steam over barely simmering water for 1 hour–1¼ hours.

After 45 minutes, check every 15 minutes to see if the custard has set. (*Do not allow it to get too hot or overcooked.*) When the custard has set, remove and leave to cool in its bowl. To serve, run a knife around the sides of the custard and turn out onto a serving dish. Spoon over any remaining caramel. Finely slice the half peach and use to border the custard.

100 g/4 oz granulated sugar
4 tablespoons cold water
600 ml/1 pint milk
3 drops almond essence
25 g/1 oz cornflour
4 eggs
4 egg yolks
3 tablespoons caster sugar
grated rind of 1 lemon
2 ripe peaches, peeled and stoned

BANANA WALNUT SLICE

This perfectly moist sponge can be served with a cup of tea or as a pudding with chopped bananas and crème anglaise.

▶ Base-line and grease a 450-g/1-lb loaf tin. Cream the butter and caster sugar until light and fluffy. Gradually add the eggs, beating well between each addition. Stir in the bananas and gently fold in the flour and nuts.

Turn into the loaf tin. Cover with a pleated piece of greased foil or greaseproof paper and tie down with string. Place in the top compartment of the steamer and steam over boiling water for 1½–2 hours. *Check the liquid level frequently and add more boiling water if necessary.* Transfer to a wire rack to cool.

Make the cream filling by mixing the bananas, sugar, lemon juice, quark, cream and walnuts together in a mixing bowl.

Split the cake in half horizontally and sandwich the layers together with the filling. Sprinkle the top of the cake with icing sugar.

100 g/4 oz butter, softened
100 g/4 oz caster sugar
2 eggs, beaten
2 large ripe bananas, crushed with a
  fork
100 g/4 oz self-raising flour
50 g/2 oz walnuts, roughly chopped
Banana cream filling
2 bananas
50 g/2 oz caster sugar
juice of 1 lemon
100 g/4 oz quark
4 tablespoons double cream
50 g/2 oz walnuts, finely chopped
icing sugar to sprinkle

GINGER SPONGES WITH HOT BUTTERSCOTCH SAUCE

115 g/4½ oz butter, softened
100 g/4 oz soft brown sugar
2 eggs, beaten
25 g/1 oz preserved ginger, finely
    chopped
2 tablespoons black treacle
½ teaspoon bicarbonate of soda
2 tablespoons milk
225 g/8 oz plain flour, sifted
½ teaspoon ground ginger
Butterscotch sauce
100 g/4 oz granulated sugar
50 g/2 oz unsalted butter
2 tablespoons water
4 tablespoons fromage frais or quark

This pudding may not be as healthy as some of the others in this chapter and shouldn't be served every day of the week, but as a treat it works wonders! The puddings can be made up to a week in advance and kept in an airtight tin, then reheated over boiling water.

▶ Grease the insides of four ramekins with 15 g/½ oz of the butter. Beat the remaining butter and the sugar together until light and fluffy. Add the eggs gradually, beating well between each addition. Stir in the preserved ginger and treacle. Mix the bicarbonate of soda with the milk and leave to one side. Fold in the sifted flour and ground ginger. Stir in the milk and bicarbonate of soda mixture.

Divide the mixture between the four ramekins. Cover with pleated pieces of foil and tie down with string. Place in a steamer. Cover with a tight fitting lid and steam over boiling water for 30 minutes. *Check the liquid level frequently and add more boiling water if necessary.*

Meanwhile make the sauce. Melt the sugar in a dry saucepan over moderate heat. Stir until the sugar has melted and the colour is golden caramel. Lower the heat and add the butter and water, stirring until the butter has melted. Leave to cool for 5 minutes. Stir in the fromage frais or quark. Keep warm over a pan of warm water. *Do not reboil.*

To serve, remove the foil and turn the sponges out on to four warmed plates. Pour over the butterscotch sauce and serve at once.

CARROT AND PECAN SPONGE

5 tablespoons clear honey
100 g/4 oz pecan nuts, roughly
    chopped
2 teaspoons fine white breadcrumbs
225 g/8 oz self-raising flour
1 teaspoon ground cinnamon
100 g/4 oz butter
100 g/4 oz sugar
225 g/8 oz carrots, finely grated

Carrots, rather like bananas, cook to produce a fabulously moist sponge brimming with vitamin C. I have chosen to use my favourite nuts for this recipe – pecan; they come from a species of North American hickory tree. If pecan nuts are difficult to find then the best substitute is walnuts.

▶ Line and grease a 450-g/1-lb loaf tin using butter. Mix together half of the honey and half of the nuts with the breadcrumbs. Spoon into the tin.

Sift the flour and cinnamon into a mixing bowl. Melt the butter, remaining honey and the sugar together in a saucepan, then stir into the flour. Add the carrots and remaining nuts. Mix well to combine thoroughly. Pile into the loaf tin. Cover with greased pleated foil and tie down with string. Steam over boiling water for 1 hour.

Remove the foil. To serve, turn the sponge out on to a serving dish and spoon over any remaining honey pecan mixture. Serve with cream, fromage frais or natural yogurt.

Steamed Nectarines with Melon Apricot Sauce (page 111);
Hot Chocolate Pudding (page 120)

STEAMED PUDDING WITH EXOTIC FRUIT SAUCE

100 g/4 oz butter, softened
100 g/4 oz caster sugar
grated rind and juice of $\frac{1}{2}$ orange
2 eggs
1 mango, peeled and stoned
75 g/3 oz raisins
100 g/4 oz self-raising flour
milk
sugared mint leaves to garnish
Sauce
1 mango, peeled and stoned
2 passion fruit, cut in half
juice of 1 orange
50 ml/2 fl oz water

Here is a light, fluffy pudding on a pool of vivid yellow fruit sauce that will warm your hearts. Use a purée of any colourful fruit if you can't get mango.

▶ Base-line and grease four deep ramekins with a little butter.

Cream the butter, sugar and orange rind together until light and fluffy. Gradually add the eggs, beating well to avoid curdling. Finely chop half the mango, reserving the remaining half for garnish. Stir in the raisins, orange juice and chopped mango. Gently fold in the flour and enough milk to make the mixture loose enough to drop from the spoon. Spoon into the ramekins. Cover each with a pleated piece of foil and tie down. Place in a steamer. Cover with a tight fitting lid and steam over boiling water for 45 minutes. *Check liquid level frequently and add more boiling water if necessary.*

Meanwhile make the sauce. Place the mango, passion fruit, orange juice and water in a food processor. Blend until smooth. Sieve to remove the passion fruit pips. The sauce can be served hot or cold.

Brush four sprigs of mint with water or egg white. Dip the leaves in a bowl of sugar. Slice the remaining half mango finely. To serve, make a pool on each plate with half of the sauce. Turn a sponge out on top of each pool. Garnish with sugared mint leaves and slices of fresh mango.

HOT CHOCOLATE PUDDING

75 g/3 oz plain chocolate
3 tablespoons milk
225 g/8 oz self-raising flour, sifted
100 g/4 oz butter, softened
50 g/2 oz caster sugar
2 eggs, beaten
caster sugar for dusting

Forget the word 'health' with this recipe. I suggest that this traditional favourite is served as an occasional treat and not every day!

As you can no doubt imagine, hot chocolate puddings go beautifully with plenty of whipped cream and chocolate sauce.

▶ Grease a 1.15-ml/2-pint pudding basin with a little butter.

Melt the chocolate gently with the milk over a pan of simmering water. Place the flour in a bowl and rub in the butter until the mixture resembles breadcrumbs. Stir in the sugar, eggs and chocolate until smooth. Add more milk if necessary to make the mixture loose enough to drop from a spoon. Turn into the prepared pudding basin. Cover with pleated greased foil or greaseproof paper and tie down with string.

Steam over boiling water for $1\frac{1}{2}$–2 hours. *Check the liquid level frequently and add more boiling water if necessary.*

Turn out on to a warmed dish. Dust with caster sugar and serve at once.

GLOSSARY OF INGREDIENTS

CHEESE

Fromage blanc Low-fat soft cheese made from skimmed milk. Available in most supermarkets.

Quark A firmer soft cheese also very low in fat. Available in supermarkets and delicatessens.

FISH AND SHELLFISH

Clams Clams are now being cultivated in Britain and look a little like flat pebbles. They are sold live in their shells, like mussels, and often served raw like oysters. They are available all year round but are of slightly better quality in the autumn.

Cod Cod vary enormously in size: the small ones are sold whole and the larger ones sold as steaks and fillets.

The flesh is firm and white and responds perfectly to steaming. Try to get fresh when possible but avoid fish that look dry and grey. Frozen cod is readily available in most supermarkets but for fresh cod, the best season is from October through to April.

Conger eel The conger eel is a popular sea eel whose flesh is firm, white and relatively sweet. For best results steam over strong fish stock. Conger eel is available fresh from March to October.

Grey mullet Grey mullet is an estuary fish that is grey with dark stripes and usually about 33–38 cm/13–15 in long. The flesh is firm and quite fatty, so try to avoid buying over-sized fish with flabby flesh. Make sure that it is thoroughly cleaned and washed, and scale the fish properly as the scales are large and indigestible. To do this efficiently you can use a fish scaler, the blunt side of a sturdy knife or a scallop shell. Lay the mullet on a work surface, hold the tail and scrape away the scales, working from the tail to the head. Grey mullet is best from July to February.

Haddock It is a member of the cod family, and is sold whole or as fillets and steaks. Although not quite as tasty as cod, it is reasonably cheap and very versatile. If you are having problems getting any fish for a particular recipe, you can always substitute firm white-fleshed haddock.

Smoked haddock is also very popular. It is smoked either on the bone or as fillets. Watch out for very yellow haddock which has probably been artificially coloured and will lose its flavour very quickly.

Fresh haddock is available all year round but is best between November and February.

Lobster Lobster is not fished in great numbers and so it remains a relatively expensive luxury.

When buying, choose a medium-sized lobster that feels heavy for its size. The males are smaller than the females but have bigger claws, however the female meat is always slightly more tender and they have broader tails. Females also contain the coral and eggs which can be made into delicious lobster butter. Whatever you choose, male or female, the tail should be resilient and spring back when straightened.

Lobsters are best when sold alive and cooked at home. It is easier to obtain the ready-cooked (and probably frozen) variety literally anywhere, but they simply do not compare in flavour with fresh lobster. To extract the meat from the cooked lobster, lay it on a chopping board, twist off the claws and legs and crack them open with a wooden rolling pin or mallet. Lay the lobster on its back and with a sharp knife cut down the middle and along the length of the lobster. Pull the halves apart and extract the meat. Discard the white gills and the grey-black thread of intestine running along the tail.

Monkfish Do not be put off by the appearance of the monkfish. It is normally sold without its head as it is so ugly! The flesh is firm and white and, when cooked, flakes into bite-sized chunky pieces. It is often used as false scampi as it is cheaper and has a flavour similar to lobster.

Mussels There are several varieties of mussels available: English, French, Dutch and Spanish. English are best in the winter months.

To clean them, wash well under cold running water. Scrape the outsides until they are free of barnacles and seaweed. Pull off the fibrous beard. Squeeze them, and if they move they are full of sand and need to be discarded. Also tap each mussel and discard any that are cracked or open. Rinse them once again under cold water, and they are then ready to use.

Plaice Another popular and slightly more economical flat fish, plaice is easily recognised by its orange-spotted upper side. When buying, make sure the spots are bright with no signs of drying out or discolouration. Plaice is sold whole or in fillets. Try to buy it without its skin, or alternatively take time to remove it as the plaice will be much nicer to eat without. The fish has a very mild flavour so needs to be well seasoned.

Red mullet The red mullet is a salt-water fish and is totally unrelated to the grey mullet. It is red skinned with a delicate, firm white flesh. Fresh mullet are in short supply and are mainly imported frozen from the Mediterranean or India; however those from India are not so good. Take care to remove the scales thoroughly as they, like those of the grey mullet, are large and indigestible.

Fresh red mullet are available between May and September.

Salmon Salmon are athletic fish that live most of their lives in the sea but travel up the river to spawn.

A good fresh salmon will have shiny silver scales and a strong pink coloured flesh. Salmon vary in size from 1.75–9 kg/4–20 lb in weight.

Try to avoid buying salmon that has been frozen as you would better off getting a piece of fresh turbot or cod. There is nothing better than a piece of beautifully cooked salmon and nothing more disappointing than the taste of the fish when overcooked.

A small salmon up to 3.5 kg/8 lb in weight is known as a grilse. Fresh salmon is available from May to July.

Salmon trout Surprisingly, salmon trout is not related to the salmon; however it has a similar firm pink-coloured flesh and delicate fine salmon flavour. It is good served either hot or cold with hollandaise or watercress mayonnaise. Average weight of the salmon trout is 1–2.75 kg/2–6 lb and they are of best quality between March and July.

Scallops There are two types of scallops you could use: the great scallop usually about 13 cm/5 in. in diameter and the much smaller queen scallop. Both are very tasty when lightly steamed. Fresh scallops are sold sitting in their shells, and frozen ones are sold without their shells.

Always use fresh whenever possible. To clean a scallop, hold the shell, hinge outwards in a cloth then carefully slide a small knife through the hinge. Twist the shell open as you slide the knife round. Cut the scallop close to the shell. Discard the green and black sac whilst rinsing under water leaving a scallop of white flesh and pink coral.

Scampi Scampi were originally caught near Dublin and are known as Dublin Bay Prawns. The French call them Langoustines. They are the largest variety of British prawn being about 10 cm/4 in long. The plump tails hold the delicious edible part. Try to buy them alive to cook at home, but ready-cooked and frozen are available. Scampi are available all year round, however, they are of the best quality between May and November.

Smoked salmon It is possible to get Scottish, Canadian, Norwegian and Pacific smoked salmon. The Scottish version has strips of fat between the meat and is the finest and most expensive. The others are slightly drier but still perfectly good.

Sole The Dover and lemon sole are both much loved members of the flat fish family. The Dover sole has olive black skin with irregular black markings, and is the most expensive of the two with the flesh finely textured and the flavour exquisite. The lemon sole has light brown skin with dark brown spots on the upperside and is slightly wider in shape. The flesh is not as delicate and the flavour, although good, is not nearly as delicious as that of the Dover sole.

Both are sold whole or as fillets, and are available all year round, however Dover sole is best between May and February and lemon sole is best between December and March.

Squid When thinking of squid, I always imagine the warm climes of Spain, Southern France or anywhere Mediterranean. British demand for squid is very small, even though large quantities are caught off the west coast of England. Cleaning a squid correctly is easy. Just cut off the head and tentacles, then put your hand into the body pouch and pull out the intestines. Remove the transparent plastic bone. Rinse well under water and peel away the outside thin film. If you cannot bear the thought of that, ask your friendly fishmonger to perform the task. But despite this, squid are tasty and versatile and well worth the effort.

Turbot In my view turbot is the most delicious of all the flat fish, but is unfortunately also one of the most expensive. It has a creamy and delicate white flesh that responds beautifully to steaming. It can be bought as steaks, fillets, or whole fish, and is available all year round but is generally best between April and July.

FRUIT

Apricot Small orange fruit with rough skin and a stone in the centre. The flesh is juicy and sweet. Choose fruit that is not too firm or bruised and squashed. They are available from May to August and December to February.

Figs Figs are mostly imported as the weather is rarely hot enough to produce the ripe, plump pear-shaped fruits, although I have spotted them growing as far north as Inverness! The flesh is sweet and heavily seeded, and the skin colour varies from purple to white with each different variety. Fresh figs are available from August to December, and dried figs are available throughout the year in most supermarkets.

Kiwi fruit Kiwi fruit are also known as Chinese gooseberries. They are egg-shaped with a brownish-green rough skin, and the inside is heavily seeded with bright green sweet tasting flesh. Although they are available all year round, the true season is from July to February.

Mango Mango is a soft spicy orange fruit with a large centre stone. The skin colour can be green, red, orange or yellow, and the size also varies enormously. Choose a firm fruit that gives slightly in the fingers when squeezed. Mangos are available from January to September.

Nectarines Nectarines are a variety of peach with a smooth shiny skin. When ripe and juicy, the flesh is orange coloured and sweet. Nectarines are available in the summer months.

Passion fruit Passion fruit has a tough skin which is dark purple and wrinkled. The flesh inside is heavily seeded but sweet and juicy: perfect for making exotic sweet sauces with mango and melon. Passion fruit is imported and available all year round.

HERBS

Basil A popular aromatic plant with juicy green leaves that originated in Italy. It is a perfect accompaniment to tomatoes.

Bay leaves Used in fresh or dried form to flavour meat or fish dishes, a bay leaf is also good in marinades, especially for fish and chicken.

Chervil A pretty green herb that is delicately flavoured; perfect for fish, chicken and vegetables.

Chives Chives are narrow-stemmed with a flavour reminiscent of onions. If not available, then use finely chopped spring onion tops.

Coriander Fresh coriander looks a little like parsley and the Indians use it as if it is parsley. It has a distinctive aroma and is used to flavour or garnish all sorts of dishes.

Dill The delicate flavour of dill complements fish perfectly and is also a popular garnish as the leaves are so pretty.

Fennel Fennel looks rather like dill but has a refreshing aniseed taste. It is a good flavouring for meat, fish and salads.

Lemon grass The presence of citric oils produce the pleasantly piquant flavour in lemon grass. Good with fish.

Marjoram A Mediterranean herb that is often linked with oregano. Marjoram has a delicate flavour and is particularly used in Italian and Spanish dishes.

Mint An excellent herb used to flavour meat, fish and vegetables as well as being a good garnish for desserts.

Parsley There are two varieties readily available in England; the flat-leaf and the curly variety. Both are superb for flavouring meat, fish and vegetable dishes, as well as being a classic and pretty garnish.

Rosemary A spiky herb with a strong flavour that is perfect for lamb and pork.

Sage A good old-fashioned herb used for stuffings and sauces. Do not use too much as the aroma can be over-powering. Perfect for chicken and pork.

Savory There are two varieties available; Winter and Summer savory. The flavour is slightly reminiscent of thyme, and you will only need to use a little as it is quite strong.

Sorrel Sorrel was one of the first herbs ever to be used and dates back to before 300 B.C. It originated from Asia and North America and became an English herb in the 13th century. Sorrel is perfect for flavouring soups and sauces and the younger leaves can be used whole in salads.

Tarragon This is one of the world's most popular herbs. The sharp but subtle aroma complements fish and chicken perfectly.

Thyme One of the most useful of all herbs, thyme helps to flavour stocks and gravies, as well as perking up bland pasta or pulse dishes. It goes very well with basil, and subtly flavours slow-cooking casseroles.

MEAT

Beef Beef should be well hung as this both improves the flavour and makes the meat more tender. Well-hung meat looks plum red in colour and should be nice and moist. Check also that it has a good covering of firm, pale yellow fat. Look for even marbling, (tiny veins of fat) as this will prevent the meat from drying out when cooked.

Cheap cuts of meat are just as nutritious as the more expensive but they need more preparation and cooking. Good cuts of beef should be served slightly underdone with a delicate deep tinge of pink at the centre.

Lamb Lamb is highly nutritious. It is a valuable source of iron, vitamins and minerals. Lamb varies in size with breed and age. The best quality is small with firm white fat. The flesh colour also varies with age and breed. Young lamb tends to have pale red meat whereas older lamb flesh is a much deeper red.

Lamb like beef benefits in flavour and texture from being hung so again find a good supplier and stick with him.

Over half of lamb in Britain is imported from Australia and New Zealand. Try to get home-produced lamb if possible as the flavour is more delicate and it does not shrink so badly when roasted. Lamb should not be served too underdone, but is perfect if the centre is tinged with pink.

Pork As people are demanding leaner cuts nowadays, pigs are slaughtered young. Look for meat that is a pinkish-white with little or no gristle. The white fat should be smooth and firm and not at all oily. Check that the bones are pinky-blue and shiny. Pork must always be well cooked to avoid any risk of infection. It contains more vitamin B_1 than any other meat and is therefore the perfect tonic for fatigue.

Veal There are two types of veal sold today: the bobby calf, which is most common in shops and has been grass fed, and the milk-fed calf, which has pale white flesh and is much more expensive.

Veal has very little fat so responds perfectly to steaming as it prevents the meat from drying out. Look for meat that is pale pink in colour with a thin covering of creamy-white fat.

The cuts of veal, and their names resemble those of a lamb rather than of grown-up beef. Take care to season the meat well as it tends to be quite bland.

Venison Venison is a word that describes the meat of any breed of deer. Try to buy the meat from a young male deer (buck) as it is better tasting and slightly more tender than that of the female. Venison should be hung for at least a week to improve the flavour and tenderise the meat.

Look for flesh that is dark red in colour and with a good covering of firm white fat. The saddle and leg joints are the best cuts and are of course the most expensive.

Venison responds well to steaming as it is usually prone to drying out if cooked badly.

Offal Most offal is highly nutritious but unfortunately, the West has become quite squeamish about it and therefore offal is given a low status among meats. Having said that, some offal such as brains, sweetbread and calf's liver are considered as delicacies.

Most offal is relatively cheap, takes little cooking and contains no fat or bones. All types of offal need to be eaten on the day of purchase as they store badly. Always keep them in the refrigerator.

Calf's brains Calf's brains need to be soaked in several changes of cold water up to 2 hours before cooking to remove traces of blood. They are loved for their glorious creamy texture, but are expensive and often difficult to get hold of. Lamb's brains can be used and are perfectly good if not quite so delicate.

Calf's liver Calf's liver has an extremely delicate and exquisite flavour. It is also the most expensive liver available. Look for meat that is pale creamy-brown and soft to the touch. Ask the butcher to remove the sinew and any inedible pipes.

Calf's sweetbreads Sweetbreads are sold in pairs being two parts of the thymus gland. They are delicate and creamy but quite expensive. If in short supply, the smaller lamb's sweetbreads make a good and inexpensive alternative. All types of sweetbreads should be soaked in several changes of water for up to 3 hours before cooking to remove any trace of blood.

Lamb's heart Lamb's hearts are the smallest of all the animal hearts. They need stuffing with interesting ingredients to add flavour. The hearts are naturally lean, so respond perfectly to steaming as this prevents the meat from drying out during cooking. Always choose bright red hearts that are firm.

Lamb's kidneys Lamb's kidneys are the most popular for everyday cooking. They have an excellent flavour that is not too strong nor bland. Look for kidneys that are light brown and firm textured.

For an expensive and exquisitely flavoured alternative use calf's kidneys. Always remove the core and sinew before cooking any kidneys.

Lamb's liver Lamb's liver is the next best thing to calf's liver and is also a lot cheaper. Look for meat that is a light reddish-brown. The flavour is good but not as delicate as the calf's.

Ox tongue Ox tongue is usually sold fresh or salted. If salted it will need to soak for up to 12 hours. Look for tongue that is soft to the touch. Remove the tough and pigmented skin after cooking or before serving.

Cooked tongue is often pressed into a round mould when hot to give it the familiar round shape.

POULTRY AND GAME

Chicken Chicken sold today are usually young and tender. Always check that they have plump white breasts, pliable breastbones and smooth legs.

They are available throughout the year fresh or frozen, and mostly sold already plucked, drawn and trussed, in other words, oven-ready. Always defrost a frozen chicken completely before cooking and remember to remove the plastic packed giblets.

Allow 225 g–350 g/8–12 oz oven-ready weight per person. Chickens are sold under different names according to their weight and age:
Poussin The name for a baby chicken usually about 4 weeks old. Allow one poussin per person. Usually about 450 g/1 lb in weight.
Double Poussin A chicken that is 6–8 weeks old and about 1 kg/2 lb in weight. Good for two people.
Spring Chicken Slightly older with an average weight of 1.25 kg/2½ lb. A good size for three portions.
Capon A young cock bird that has been castrated. Good full flavour meat. About 2.75–3.5 kg/6–8 lb in weight.
Boiling Fowl A hen bird that has completed the laying season. It is a fatty bird but the meat is very tasty. Boiling fowl is excellent for slower cooking, but these days needs to be ordered in advance.

Duck Domestic duck are fatty birds. The fat is situated under the skin and can be completely removed before cooking. However, if you are roasting, do not remove the skin as the fat bastes the bird during cooking and keeps it succulent.

The most famous breed of duck is the Aylesbury, with an average weight of 1.75–2.75 kg/4–6 lb. You will need a 2.75-kg/6-lb bird when serving four people. Duck is available all year round

fresh and frozen, but is best of all fresh from August to December.

Duckling is obviously smaller with an average weight of 1.5–1.75 kg/3–4 lb and each one will only serve two people. Duckling is of best quality fresh from April to July. Steaming prevents the flesh from drying out during cooking and retains all the valuable nutrients and flavour.

Mallard duck is commonly described as wild duck and should not be associated with its domestic cousins in either flavour or meat-to-bone ratio. The wastage on wild duck is infinitely less, and in terms of flavour it is indescribably delicious and rich alongside domestic ducks. Wild duck is of best quality from September to December.

The teal duck is a smaller cousin of the mallard, and is just as well flavoured.

Grouse Grouse are hardy moorland birds which come into season earlier than any other game bird. August the 12th is the opening day and grouse are available fresh until December.

The flesh is exquisitely flavoured and the younger birds need only a short cooking time. Serve one bird per person.

Guinea fowl Guinea fowl are now bred for the table and available all year round. They are also known as squab. The U.K. production of the bird is not sufficient to meet popular demand so some are imported from Europe, frozen and oven-ready.

The flesh is white and the mild flavour will offend nobody. One bird will serve two people.

Pheasant Cock and hen pheasants when sold together are called a brace, as with many other game birds, but are easily available singly. Try to get young birds with soft pliable beaks and feet. I think that hen birds are often better tasting as well as being generally cheaper. The hen will serve three people and the cock will serve four.

Turkey Despite its reputation as a Christmas bird, turkey is available all year round. With an average weight of 4.5–6.25 kg/10–14 lb per bird, it is very economical for large family meals or parties. You should allow 350 g/12 oz per person if roasting the turkey. Although turkey is often notorious for drying out during cooking, steaming it gently in foil guarantees succulent results.

If you have the choice, try to buy hen birds as they have plumper breasts and smaller legs. You can substitute turkey for any recipe that uses chicken, and cooking times will still be the same, pound for pound.

Wood pigeon Wood pigeon have been long underrated in this country but now appear regularly on restaurant menus, and are cheap and easily available. When properly hung, the firm meat has a strong flavour. Serve one bird per person. They are available all year round but are best from August to October.

PULSES

Butter beans Traditionally these beans came from Madagascar but nowadays the American lima bean has become more popular.

Butter beans are a valuable source of protein, fibre and minerals and have the added advantage of being low in fat. Soak them overnight, drain, rinse and boil in clean water for 20 minutes or until soft.

Chick peas These are medium-sized round peas with a distinctive yellow gold colour and nutty flavour. Soak overnight, rinse and boil for 1 hour or until soft.

Fermented black beans These are smallish black beans, usually soy, with a surface wrinkled by fermentation in salt. Much used in Chinese cooking, they are available in packets or cans from Chinese supermarkets.

Red kidney beans These are medium-sized beans that have a distinctive red colour. They are mostly imported from the U.S.A. and are popular in hot spicy dishes. Soak them overnight, drain, rinse and boil for 40 minutes or until soft. Like most pulses, kidney beans *must* be boiled for at least 10 minutes to destroy the poisonous enzymes; canned kidney beans however are perfectly safe.

Split lentils These are tiny orange or yellow discs that do not need to be presoaked. They turn to mush when cooked so are perfect for purées and pâtés. Pick them over to remove any black grit, then rinse and boil them for 15 minutes.

RICE AND OTHER GRAINS

Rice Rice is one of man's oldest crops. The first record of its cultivation dates back as far as 5000 BC and over half of the world's population depends on rice for its staple diet. America is now the world's major exporter. Make sure the rice is washed in several bowls of water until the liquid is clear, before steaming. Do not use easy-cook rice for steaming as it lacks the starchy flavour and texture needed for perfect results.

Basmati Basmati is a high quality fine-grain rice grown in Pakistan and India. The flavour is distinctive and the rice is more dense in colour.

Patna Patna is another variety of long-grain white rice which is cheap and readily available everywhere.

Bulgar Bulgar has a variety of names so look out for 'cracked wheat', 'burghul' or 'pourgouri'. It has a good nutty flavour, and makes an ideal alternative to rice, and is available in plenty of health shops and supermarkets.

Cornmeal Like bulgar, cornmeal has other names: it is also called 'polenta' or 'maizemeal'. It is a distinctive bright yellow colour with a delicious nutty flavour, and you can get medium or fine grain cornmeal; either will do for cooking. If using the medium grain, then the texture will be a little more gritty but still just as good.

Couscous A type of semolina popular in North Africa and France: see recipe in chapter on Pasta, Pulses & Grains.

Semolina Semolina is an intermediate product of flour milling. It can be made from all types of wheat but the best quality is undoubtedly that which is milled from 100% durum wheat; this is recognised by the yellow tinge and sharp granules.

SPICES

Cardamom An essential spice for Indian cooking. It is a small green pod containing tiny black seeds, and is used to flavour sweet and savoury dishes. The seeds can be removed and used for cooking, or you can use the whole pod but you must remove it before eating.

Cayenne Cayenne is made from dried red chillies and is therefore very powerful and hot!

Cinnamon Try to buy cinnamon sticks as they can be used whole for cooking sweet and savoury dishes, then washed, dried and used once or twice more. They are not meant for eating! Ground cinnamon can also be used as the results are just as good.

Cloves Cloves can be used whole or ground. If cooking with whole cloves, remove them from the food before eating.

Coriander Coriander seeds can be sold whole or ground, and used to flavour Far Eastern dishes. Coriander goes particularly well with carrots!

Cumin seeds These are also sold whole or ground. The whole seeds keep their flavour for much longer when stored.

Ginger Fresh ginger is a peculiar-shaped knobbly plant with a tough skin and pungent flesh. Remove the skin, and grate the ginger for cooking.

Ground ginger is simply ginger that has been dried and powdered, and is used in both sweet and savoury dishes.

Nutmeg Buy whole nutmegs when possible as the flavour is always fresher, and you can grate what you want when you need it.

Paprika A bright red powder that comes from the same family as cayenne. It is a Hungarian spice and its sweet, mild flavour is added to the classic dishes of goulash and stroganoff.

Saffron Saffron is the dried stamens of a special breed of crocus, and is extremely expensive. It is used in Indian festival dishes. In its place, yellow food colouring, or a small pinch of turmeric, works just as well.

VEGETABLES

Asparagus Asparagus are expensive since during most of the year they are imported, and the English season is only May and June. When buying, look for buds that are tightly closed and have a good green colour with some bleached or white parts showing. Avoid fat asparagus stalks as they will be very fibrous, and also avoid thin, woody dry stems as they will be too tough and stringy.

Green asparagus has been grown in sunlight and white is grown away from sunlight, often underground. Use both where possible as the beauty of the ingredients is a major contribution to the enjoyment of the dish.

Aubergine Often known as eggplant, aubergine is a long pear-shaped vegetable easily recognised by its distinctive shiny, purple, firm skin. The flesh is greenish-yellow and soft when cooked. Aubergines are readily available all year round.

Celeriac Celeriac is a root vegetable and a member of the celery family. It has a brown fibrous skin and white flesh. The flesh discolours in air unless brushed with lemon juice, and it goes gluey if puréed in a liquidiser or food processor. Celeriac vary from apple to coconut size and are usually available during the winter.

Fennel Fennel has a distinct aniseed flavour and looks rather like a swollen root or bulb. It is greenish-white in colour and readily available all year round. Try to buy bulbs with leaves on, as you can use the leaves as herbs to flavour fish and chicken.

Horseradish Fresh horseradish is a root and not a vegetable, but can be peeled and grated to make a strong-flavoured sauce. It is available throughout the autumn and winter months.

Jerusalem artichokes A peculiar shaped vegetable that looks like a knobbly root with an off-white-purple skin. The flesh is white and discolours in air unless brushed with lemon juice. It is delicately flavoured, and perfect for soups, or as a vegetable accompaniment to chicken and fish.

Kohlrabi A root with a distinctive purple coloured skin. The flavour is reminiscent of turnip, and you should aim to get smaller roots as they are sweet and tender. Kohlrabi are available from July all the way through to April.

Pumpkin Pumpkin can be as heavy as 100 lb and are thankfully sold in pieces! Try to buy flesh that is smooth, not stringy, and has a fresh orange colour. They are available from June to October.

Salsify They always look dirty but the dark brown outside skin is deceptive. Salsify is a root with a delicious white flesh and a flavour that complements meat and chicken. It is available throughout the winter months.

Shallots Shallots are miniature onions with a slight garlic flavour, perfect for sauces and marinades. Make sure you choose tight round bulbs. They are available throughout autumn and winter.

Sweet potatoes Sweet potatoes are usually long and elongated although the odd roundish one might appear from time to time. They have reddish skin and are not related to ordinary potatoes, other than that they are both root vegetables. The sweet potato flesh is yellow-orange and when cooked is soft and sweet. They are available from November to March.

INDEX